THE HOME FRONT 1939-45

Nicholas Williams
Deputy Head of The Netherhall School, Cambridge

Nelson

For my mother and father

Thomas Nelson and Sons Ltd
Nelson House Mayfield Road
Walton-on-Thames Surrey
KT12 5PL UK

Nelson Blackie
Wester Cleddens Road
Bishopbriggs
Glasgow
G64 2NZ UK

Thomas Nelson (Hong Kong) Ltd
Toppan Building 10/F
22a Westlands Road
Quarry Bay Hong Kong

Thomas Nelson Australia
102 Dodds Street
South Melbourne
Victoria 3205 Australia

Nelson Canada
1120 Birchmount Road
Scarborough Ontario
M1K 5G4 Canada

First published by Macmillan Education Ltd 1990
(under ISBN 0-333-48525-4)

This edition published by Thomas Nelson and Sons Ltd 1994

I(T)P Thomas Nelson is an International
Thomson Publishing Company.

I(T)P is used under licence.

ISBN 0-17-435153-4
NPN 9 8 7 6 5 4 3 2

Printed in China

Author's acknowledgements
The author would like to thank Ruth Vincent of the Imperial War Museum and Mike Petty of the Cambridgeshire Collection for their assistance with research.

CONTENTS

Acknowledgements

The author and publishers wish to thank the following who have kindly given permission for the use of copyright material:

The Controller of Her Majesty's Stationery Office for material from 'Front Line', 1940–42, and a 1936 report, COI; Methuen & Co. for material from *Cambridge Evacuation Survey* by Susan Isaacs, 1941; Solo Syndication Ltd. for material from the *Daily Mail*, October 1942; Syndication International Ltd. for material from the *Daily Mirror*, 5 February 1942.

The author and publishers wish to acknowledge, with thanks, the following photographic sources:

BBC Hulton Picture Company pp 5, 7, 16, 17, 21, 30 top, 32, 34, 35, 43, 52–3, 53 bottom right, 54 bottom right, 62 top, 68; Cambridgeshire Collection, Cambridgeshire Libraries pp 10–11, 50; Cambridge University Library p 22; Imperial War Museum pp 16–17, 19, 25, 53 top, 67 both; Manchester Public Library p 8; Popperfoto pp 24, 36, 39, 41, 62 bottom left; *Punch* pp 49, 56–7, 65, 66; Topham Photograph Library pp 44, 45, 53 centre, 53 bottom left, 54 top left, 54 top right, 54 bottom left; N. Williams p 33.

Every effort has been made to trace all the copyright holders, but if any have been inadvertently overlooked the publishers will be pleased to make the necessary arrangements at the first opportunity.

PREFACE

The study of history is exciting, whether in a good story well told, a mystery solved by the judicious unravelling of clues, or a study of the men, women and children whose fears and ambitions, successes and tragedies make up the collective memory of mankind.

This series aims to reveal this excitement to pupils through a set of topic books on important historical subjects from the Middle Ages to the present day. Each book contains four main elements: a narrative and descriptive text, lively and relevant illustrations, extracts of contemporary evidence, and questions for further thought and work. Involvement in these elements should provide an adventure which will bring the past to life in the imagination of the pupil.

Each book is also designed to develop the knowledge, skills and concepts so essential to a pupil's growth. It provides a wide, varying introduction to the evidence available on each topic. In handling this evidence, pupils will increase their understanding of basic historical concepts such as causation and change, as well as of more advanced ideas such as revolution and democracy. In addition, their use of basic study skills will be complemented by more sophisticated historical skills such as the detection of bias and the formulation of opinion.

The intended audience for the series is pupils of eleven to sixteen years; it is expected that the earlier topics will be introduced in the first three years of secondary school, while the nineteenth and twentieth century topics are directed towards first examinations.

1

WAR BEGINS

Early on the morning of 1 September 1939, German forces invaded Poland. The British Government had already promised to support Poland against any future attack. At 11.15 a.m. on Sunday, 3 September, Neville Chamberlain, the British Prime Minister, made a radio broadcast to the nation:

> *This morning, the British Ambassador in Berlin handed the German Government a final note, stating that unless the British Government heard from them by 11 o'clock that they were prepared at once to withdraw their troops from Poland, a state of war would exist between us. I have to tell you now that no such undertaking has been received and that consequently this country is at war with Germany.*

War is declared. The white bands on the trees were a precaution against blackout accidents (see Chapter 4).

The air-raid sirens sounded almost immediately, but it was a false alarm. The expected bomber attacks on British towns and cities did not begin for almost a year. Even so, the old peacetime way of life soon disappeared. Men were conscripted into the armed forces, women and children were evacuated from danger zones, road signs and railway station names were removed, and a night-time blackout was imposed. No one imagined that the war would drag on for nearly six years. Few people understood that the whole nation – men, women and children – were about to engage in a life and death struggle. This war would be fought, in different ways, in the factories, in the streets, and even in the kitchens of Britain. Just as there would be battlefronts in various parts of the world, with soldiers fighting each other, so there would be a different type of battlefront in Britain – called the Home Front. Here civilians would work to produce supplies and weapons to equip the armed forces; they would struggle against shortages and hunger; and they would face terrifying attacks from the air.

In the summer of 1940, Winston Churchill, the new Prime Minister, paid tribute to the unsung heroes and heroines of the Home Front:

> *This is a war of the unknown warriors. . . . The whole of the warring nations are engaged, not only soldiers, but the entire population, men, women and children. The fronts are everywhere. The trenches are dug in the towns and streets. Every village is fortified. Every road is barred. The front lines run through the factories. The workmen are soldiers with different weapons, but the same courage.*

2 EVACUATION

If we were involved in a war, our big cities might be subjected to determined attacks from the air – at any rate in the early stages – and although our defences are strong and rapidly growing stronger, some bombers would undoubtedly get through.

We must see to it then that the enemy does not secure his chief objects – the creation of anything like panic, or the crippling dislocation of our civil life.

One of the first measures we can take to prevent this is the removal of the children from the more dangerous areas. . . . You cannot wish, if it is possible to evacuate them, to let your children experience the dangers and fears of air attack in crowded cities.

Evacuation: Why and How, Public Information Leaflet No. 3, July 1939

The government believed that the declaration of war would immediately be followed by German air attacks on British towns and cities. Cinema newsreels of the Spanish Civil War had warned the public just how devastating such attacks could be. There was already widespread fear and, when the air raids began, this fear might turn into mass civilian panic. Thus, with the approach of war, the government made plans for the official evacuation of 'priority classes' – children

Schoolchildren leaving Blackhorse Road station, London, 1 September 1939.

and women with babies – from the danger areas. For this purpose, it divided Britain into three zones:

a) **Evacuation areas** – these were towns and cities that could expect heavy air raids and so should be cleared of children, pregnant women and mothers with babies.
b) **Reception areas** – these were considered relatively safe from enemy attack and therefore suitable to receive evacuees from other areas.
c) **Neutral areas** – these might suffer light attacks; they should neither send nor receive evacuees.

From January 1939 volunteers investigated surplus accommodation in the 'safe' areas and reported that they could cope with up to 4 800 000 evacuees. The government ordered the construction of a number of emergency camps to provide some additional accommodation. Posters and leaflets were hurriedly printed and circulated, urging parents to register their children for evacuation. Finally, much time and energy were spent organising public and private transport, so that when the time for evacuation arrived millions of children could be removed to the countryside in just a few days.

The evacuation programme began on 1 September 1939. Over the next four days the railway companies carried over 1 300 000 official evacuees in nearly 4000 special trains. The London buses also performed miracles. They transported nearly a quarter of a million

The evacuation of children from Manchester, September 1939.

passengers to the railway stations or direct to their new homes. Of course there were problems. Some of the trains lacked canteens and toilets, with the result that many children reached their destination hungry and soiled. Some children arrived at the wrong destination. But, on the whole, this phase of the evacuation programme was a model of efficiency.

> *London was early astir for the great evacuation. Before dawn teachers, marshals and officials were making their way to the schools to prepare for their big task. . . .*
>
> *Each child, whose ages ranged from 3 to 13, carried a gas mask, food and a change of clothing, and bore three labels. They all received strict instructions from the head teacher 'Not to suck or eat your labels'.*
>
> *. . . They were a very cheerful crowd of youngsters, though a few had evidently shed some tears at the parting with their parents.*
>
> *Cambridge Daily News*, 1 September 1939

> *Everyone was singing: 'There'll always be an England' and such Gracie Fields hits as we could remember. I was vomiting out of the bus window as the convoy of buses wove its way through Sherwood Forest, my sister Peggy keeping her arm round me. Brian, who was the youngest at five years of age, normally a terror and a tearabout, sat quiet and saying nothing at this sudden unexpected upheaval.*
>
> Alan Sillitoe, quoted in *Children and the War*, ed. A. Calder, 1973

Questions

1 Examine the extract from the Public Information Leaflet at the beginning of this chapter.
   a) What appears to be the government's main reason for evacuating children from threatened towns and cities?
   b) Which passage in this leaflet seems to be trying to reassure the public that Britain is well prepared to meet the German attacks?
   c) If you were the parent of young children, would this leaflet persuade you to evacuate them? Give reasons for your answer.

2 Look again at the two accounts of children being evacuated.
   a) In what ways do these two accounts agree and how do they differ?
   b) The newspaper report was written on the day of the events it describes. Alan Sillitoe's account was written many years later. Does that make the newspaper account a more reliable source of evidence on evacuation? Explain your answer.

Above: *evacuees from London arriving at Cambridge station. What information do you suppose was written on the children's labels?*

3 Copy the map of Britain in 1939 into your exercise book. Using different coloured pencils, shade in the areas that you think were probably evacuation, reception and neutral zones.
Compare your finished map with those done by others in the class and discuss how you reached your decisions.

Arrival

The real problems began when the evacuees arrived at their reception areas, most of which found themselves welcoming far fewer evacuees than they had expected. Cambridge, for example, was expecting 24 000 evacuees but received only 6700. This was because the government's campaign to persuade parents to part with their children had been only partly successful. Whereas 70 per cent of the children were evacuated from Manchester, only 15 per cent left Sheffield. An

Above right: *evacuees receiving their rations on arrival at Cambridge.*

additional problem was that some reception areas did not receive the evacuees they had been promised. Communities expecting to care for young children sometimes found themselves having to house hordes of pregnant women instead! But the major problem arose from the inefficiency of some of the local authorities in reception areas. They failed to make adequate plans to cope with even the reduced number of evacuees. Very few authorities matched the efficiency of Cambridge. Here evacuated children were greeted with a carrier bag containing a tin of meat, two tins of milk, a packet of biscuits and some chocolates. They were then quickly taken to their billets.

In some other areas, however, tired children were left waiting around for hours. Then there was a free-for-all with local people assembling on station platforms to pick their evacuees. It was rather like a cattle market or an auction.

> *My sisters were crying because women were pulling them this way and that. My brother and I were dragged by one woman up against a wall, and another woman was fighting her for my brother. We were torn from our homes, shipped all over the country and ended up seemingly on an auction block.*
>
> Quoted in B. Wicks' book, *No Time to Wave Goodbye*, 1988

Even worse problems were to follow when the evacuees reached their new homes. The government had simply been concerned with sending

Bombed-out children from London 'on display' at a reception area.

children and mothers with babies to safe areas and finding them temporary billets. It had not anticipated the social problems that would result. The limited sanitary, health and social amenities of the countryside were soon swamped by this invasion from the towns. Evacuees billeted on farm labourers were often horrified to discover that their water had to be fetched from a well and their lavatory was the surrounding fields! In addition, children and mothers used to the noise, traffic, shops and entertainments of the towns were confused and even frightened by the peace and quiet of remote villages.

A still more worrying problem was the inability of many evacuees and their hosts to understand each other. This resulted from the fact that while most evacuees came from the densely populated, poorer districts of cities, the people in the countryside with spare rooms in their homes were often quite well-off farmers and professional people. It followed that poor children from slum districts sometimes found themselves billeted in comfortable, middle-class homes. This could produce all sorts of tensions. But painful though this experience was, it did at least force many middle-class people to take notice of the grinding poverty of the working classes. Middle-class complaints about the poor clothing, inadequate diet and verminous state of many working-class evacuees finally persuaded the government to act. Money was paid to education authorities for the re-clothing of some children. The government also provided more hostels, social amenities, welfare centres, residential nurseries, canteens and social workers in reception areas. In this way the evacuation experiment actually resulted in a new government concern for the welfare of its poorer citizens.

Using the evidence

Many evacuees quickly adapted to their new surroundings and formed close relationships with their rural hosts. Sometimes these friendships lasted for many years after the war. In other cases there was continuing friction and even hostility. After all, this was the first time that the town and the countryside, the poor and the rich, had been forced to live together. For some people this was not a particularly happy experience. The following sources reflect the two extreme points of view. They illustrate what could happen when slum children were evacuated to more prosperous country areas.

The hosts' view

A *I got a shock. I had little dreamt that English children could be so completely ignorant of the simplest rules of hygiene, and that they would regard the floors and carpets as suitable places upon which to relieve themselves.*

The Memoirs of Lord Chandos, 1962

B *Except for a small number the children were filthy, and in this district we have never seen so many verminous children lacking any knowledge of clean and hygienic habits. Furthermore, it appeared they were unbathed for months. One child was suffering from scabies and the majority had it in their hair and the others had dirty septic sores all over their bodies.*

National Federation of Women's Institutes: *Town Children Through Country Eyes*, 1940

C *A WVS Billeting Officer in Cornwall had to cope with an angel-faced five-year-old from an Irish docker's family in the East End of London who electrified a respectable farmer's family by casually remarking when she dropped a fork, 'Blast that f—ing b——!' When told off she answered, 'I'll tell my dad about you and he'll come and knock your bleeding block off.'*

Norman Longmate: *How We Lived Then*, 1971

D *The first morning I was awoken about 6 a.m. by such a noise, it was the boys [two evacuees] fighting in bed! One had a bloody nose which had splattered all over the wall. I cleaned them up and got them ready for breakfast. They had no idea how to use a knife and fork and picked up a fried egg in their fingers.*

Quoted in B. Wicks' book, *No Time to Wave Goodbye*, 1988

The evacuees' view

E *We were even given flannels and toothbrushes. We'd never cleaned our teeth up till then. And hot water came from the tap. And there was a lavatory upstairs. And carpets. And something called an eiderdown. And clean sheets. This was all very odd. And rather scaring.*

B. Kops: *The World is a Wedding*, 1963

F These extracts are from essays written by evacuees from Tottenham on what they disliked about Cambridge:

Boy, aged 12 – What I miss in Cambridge is the thick fogs and fish and chips.

Boy, aged 14 – I miss getting hidings from my dad when I get into trouble.

Boy, aged 13 – I miss a decent and regular bus service. I miss films that have any resemblance of being new.

Girl, aged 14 – I think the shops down here are awful, you can never get what you want.

Girl, aged 10 – There are not many parks with swings, seesaws and roundabouts.

S. Isaacs: *The Cambridge Evacuation Survey*, 1941

G *'There is nothing to do in this dump.' This is a phrase one hears over and over again. . .from everyone who has been brought into the village, more or less involuntarily, for the duration of the war.*

Mass Observation survey on evacuees in a Gloucestershire village, 1943

H *Stanley [aged 10, from Merseyside] was evacuated to Hexham, but returned after a fortnight. Some Hexham kids pushed him backwards into a cowpat. The woman he was billeted with didn't wash his blazer, and he had to go to school with the dry cowpat stuck to him, and she didn't clean his shoes or make his bed or anything. And the teacher kept remarking how scruffy town kids were. So he came home; he said it was all cows and cowpats and boring.*

Quoted in R. Westall's book, *Children of the Blitz*, 1985

1 What aspects of the evacuees' behaviour and appearance did people in reception areas find most unpleasant?

2 Make a list of all the things evacuees disliked or found strange about their temporary homes.

3 Which of the two groups – the evacuees or their hosts – do you have more sympathy for? Give reasons for your answer, then discuss your views with other members of the class.

4 Copy the following table into your exercise book. It lists several of the worst aspects of the life of the poor in Britain in the 1930s. Next to each aspect, write down the evidence from the above sources that illustrates it.

Aspects of the life of the poor	*Evidence*
Slum housing	
Lack of proper sanitation	
Limited diet	
Inadequate medical care	
Poor hygiene	
Neglect of children	

5 Imagine that you have been evacuated from the East End of London and have just arrived at your new home in a Cambridge village. Write a postcard to your parents describing your first impressions.

6 Divide the class into 'family groups' of four or five pupils. Each family is made up of Mum, Granny and two or three teenage children. Dad is away in the Army. You have a spare bedroom in your house and the local Billeting Officer has suggested that you should take in an evacuee, but your friends have told you alarming stories about the appearance and behaviour of some of these city children. You must told a family conference to discuss what to do. When you have reached a decision, write it down along with your reasons. Then discuss your family's decision with other families in the class.

Gains and losses

By 8 January 1940, 900 000 of the 1 500 000 adults and children officially evacuated in September 1939 had returned home. Many children had certainly gained something from their few months in the countryside. Some London parents reported that their children were more polite and courteous on their return home. Teachers often commented on the improved health of the children as a result of the fresh air and the better diet. Some children even developed a lasting love of the countryside:

I got my love of the country from this time – it was the first time I had ever lived in the country and I was very well fed. We had plenty of eggs, butter and milk.

Angela Sexton's memories of her evacuation to Yorkshire, quoted in Alastair and Anne Pike's book, *The Home Front in Britain*, 1985

However, there was no disguising the fact that the evacuation programme had failed. The extent of this failure was revealed in February 1940, after the start of heavy air raids, when the government introduced a new scheme to evacuate children. Only 2 per cent of householders in reception areas volunteered to accept evacuees and only 20 per cent of children in the danger zones were registered for evacuation. All future evacuation schemes, even after the start of the Blitz (see Chapter 4), met strong opposition.

Going home

The first evacuees to return home were usually the mothers with babies and toddlers. They had never been as welcome in the reception areas as the children and they had found it harder to adapt to life with 'no chip shop, no pictures, no pawnshops'. They had also found it difficult sharing a kitchen with another woman. But, most importantly, '. . . it was the loneliness of the husbands and the fear of "the woman round the corner" which sent mothers with young children back to London'.

The schoolchildren often did not stay long either. The main single cause of their return home was quite simply the fact that no bombs fell on the cities for several months after the outbreak of war. Other reasons were that many parents were dissatisfied with their children's foster homes, while some worried about the damage done to their education. Several evacuated schools had to share buildings with other schools and operate a 'shift' system. One London school which was moved to Cambridge actually had to put one of its classes in one half of a hall, while the other half was occupied by off-duty air-raid wardens continuously playing the wireless, ping pong and billiards.

Some parents brought their children home because of the financial strain. On 14 September 1939 the government finally made it clear that the parents of evacuated children would have to pay a contribution towards the cost of their keep. The exact scale of the payment would be decided by a 'means test' – an assessment of each family's ability to pay. Parents were never asked to pay more than 6s. per child per week. However, even this was too much for some families, since the average weekly earnings for men were only about £4 10s. 0d., and 'extras' such as train fares, postage and clothing had to be paid for, too. A social worker described the worry this extra expense caused in one family:

Conversion Chart

6d.	=	2½p
1s.	=	5p
2s.	=	10p
5s.	=	25p
10s.	=	50p
15s.	=	75p
20s.	=	£1

This was the *rate* at which shillings (s.) and pence (d.) were converted to decimal pence (p). Inflation means that the *value* of money has since changed, of course.

The sinister figure of Adolf Hitler tries to tempt a mother to return her children to their city home. Not even this government poster could persuade most mothers to leave their children in the care of strangers for very long.

In December 1939 the railway companies introduced cheap excursions to reception areas. These helped poorer parents to visit their evacuated children. Here children rush to welcome their parents on the arrival of the special train at Northampton station.

I have seen an unemployed father in tears because of a son's letter home saying that, while he knew his father could not spend the ten shillings demanded by the hostess for clothing, he would rather come home than endure the situation any longer.

R. Padley and M. Cole (eds): *Evacuation Survey*, 1940

Most parents brought their children home for a combination of different reasons. But once they had their children home, not even the Blitz could persuade some parents to part with them again.

Using the evidence

The table on page 18, from the Cambridge Evacuation Survey, 1941, illustrates the reasons given by a cross-section of Tottenham and Islington parents for bringing their children home:

Reasons for return	*Totals*	
	Tottenham	*Islington*
I. *Family relationships*	23	33
1. Parents anxious or lonely.	8	17
2. Child homesick or eager to return. (See 11.)	11	11
3. Parents' visits disturbing.	–	1
4. Returned because of brother or sister.	4	4
II. *Economic*	9	16
5. Billeting cost (actual or prospective).	7	12
6. Child's wages or help needed.	2	4
III. *Reception conditions*	27	18
7. Billet unsatisfactory.	18	11
8. Change of billet (actual or prospective).	9	7
IV. *The child*	10	9
9. Illness or accident.	8	5
10. Nervous or difficult.	2	2
11. Homesick. (See 2.)	–	–
12. Companions: misses or quarrels.	–	2
V. *Other reasons*	1	5
13. School unsatisfactory or inaccessible.	–	–
14. Returned for holidays.	–	5
15. Unclassified.	1	–
Total	70	81

1 What appears to be the single most important reason for bringing children home?

2 List the relatively unimportant reasons which account for only a few returns.

3 Does this table support or contradict the reasons for return given in the rest of this chapter? Explain your answer.

4 Do you think that this table is reliable? Try to think of reasons why some parents might not have been prepared to tell the researchers their real reasons for bringing their children home.

3

THE KITCHEN FRONT

Shortages

Britain could not produce enough food or raw materials to meet the needs of the population, and therefore depended on imports from overseas. As soon as the war began, German submarines and battleships began attacking merchant shipping bringing these vital supplies. It was not long before the British people began to suffer shortages of food, clothing, fuel and other raw materials. As some foods became scarce, prices rose:

> *[27 October 1939.] Prices are slowly going up. The twopenny bars of chocolate are to be smaller and restricted to standard lines, i.e. milk, plain and with or without nuts.... Sausages are now 7d. a pound – beef, that is. The makers say that skins now cost them more.... Bread is up ½d. a quartern. Lyle's Golden Syrup unobtainable....Bacon about 1s. 8d.*
>
> George Beardmore: *Civilians at War, Journals 1938–46*, 1984

a quartern: a loaf weighing 1600 grams.

The government was expecting this to happen and had been making plans for the possible introduction of food rationing since November 1936. Ration books were actually ready for issue by 1938. However, when war broke out the government was strangely reluctant to put its measures into action. This was largely because it feared the opposition of businessmen as well as the trade unions to the introduction of controls on the supply and distribution of essential goods. For the first few months of the war nothing was done. Prices continued to rise. Some wealthy people began touring the country by car, paying almost any price for 'shortage foods' which they could then hoard at home. Most people complained that this was not fair. As a result the government finally introduced food rationing on 8 January 1940. In that morning's newspapers Ministry of Food advertisements explained the reasons for rationing:

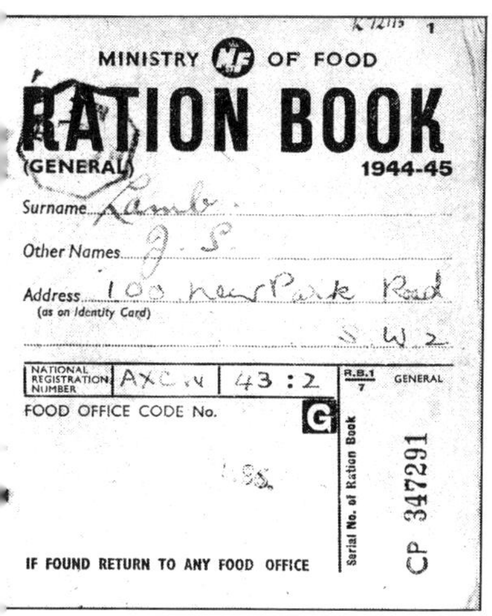
MINISTRY OF FOOD
RATION BOOK
(GENERAL) 1944-45
Surname Lamb
Other Names J. S.
Address 100 New Park Road S.W.2
(as on Identity Card)
NATIONAL REGISTRATION NUMBER AXC 43 : 2
R.B.1 GENERAL
FOOD OFFICE CODE No. G
Serial No. of Ration Book CP 347291
IF FOUND RETURN TO ANY FOOD OFFICE

After 8 January 1940 housewives were expected to use their ration books. These had been issued in September 1939.

Reasons for Rationing

1. *Rationing prevents waste of food. We must not ask our sailors to bring us unnecessary food cargoes at the risk of their lives.*
2. *Rationing increases our war effort. Our shipping carries food, and armaments in their raw and finished state, and other essential raw materials for home consumption and the export trade. To reduce our purchases of food abroad is to release ships for bringing us other imports. So we shall strengthen our war effort.*
3. *Rationing divides supplies equally. There will be ample supplies for our 44½ million people, but we must divide them fairly, everyone being treated alike. No one must be left out.*

4. *Rationing prevents uncertainty. Your ration book assures you of your fair share. Rationing means that there will be no uncertainty and no queues.*

Cambridge Daily News, 8 January 1940

Most people welcomed the introduction of food rationing:

The arrival of 'Coupon Monday', with the introduction of rationing, is welcomed in many parts of the country. People feel that it will put an end to any favouritism that may have been shown.

Every man, woman and child in the country, from the members of the Royal Family to their humblest subjects, has a ration card, which will now be worth its weight in gold to the hungry.

Cambridge Daily News, 8 January 1940

Questions

1 Explain in your own words what the Ministry of Food saw as the main reasons for introducing rationing.

2 Which of these reasons was probably of most importance to the government? Explain your answer.

3 Which of these reasons was probably of most importance to ordinary people? Explain your answer.

4 Which words and phrases in the Ministry of Food advertisement show that the government was trying to reassure the public and calm their fears?

Rationing

Rationing was an attempt to ensure that everyone, whether rich or poor, received their fair share of goods that were in short supply. At first only a limited number of essential foods were rationed. After 8 January 1940 each person was entitled to 4 oz. (100 g.) of butter, 4 oz. (100 g.) of bacon or ham, and 12 oz. (350 g.) of sugar a week. These quantities varied as the war progressed. Meat rationing followed on 11 March and in July tea, margarine and cooking fats were added to the list of rationed foods. At first many 'luxury' foods, such as tinned salmon, were left unrationed. However, people complained that only the rich were getting these items. In an attempt to correct this, the Ministry of Food introduced a points rationing scheme in December 1941. This meant that every holder of a ration card now received 16 points, later increased to 20, to spend as they liked wherever they liked. At first only canned meat, fish and vegetables were 'on points', but over the next year a range of other foods was added.

Queuing for food and other articles in short supply was one of the miseries of wartime.

It was not only food that was rationed. Clothes rationing was introduced in June 1941 and soap rationing followed in February 1942. Petrol rationing actually began as early as September 1939, but in July 1942 the basic petrol ration was abolished altogether except for those who could prove that a car or motorcycle was essential to their work.

Rationing was to remain in force for some items until well after the end of the war. Meat was the last thing to be de-rationed in June 1954. Rationing left mixed memories – of going hungry, of queuing for everything, of discovering strange substitutes for favourite foods.

The government's role

The Ministry of Food was responsible for organising rationing. This was a massive job. By 1943 the Ministry employed 50 000 civil servants. There was more to rationing than simply fixing individual food quotas. It also involved investigating the nation's diet and eating habits. For the first time ever, the government took a keen interest in the feeding of its citizens. If people were going to be asked to work hard for long hours, it was important that they should be well fed.

The government took special measures to provide for mothers, children, babies and invalids. In 1940 they introduced the National Milk Scheme, providing free milk for the poorest mothers and children. In December 1941 the Vitamin Welfare Scheme began the free issue of cod-liver oil and blackcurrant juice (later orange juice) to all children under the age of two. The government also increased the supply of free school meals. The number of children receiving these meals grew from 250 000 before the war to 1 850 000 by 1945. Great care was taken to ensure the nutritional value of all school meals.

Efforts were also made to improve the diet of adults. The government encouraged local authorities to set up Communal Feeding Centres (later re-named British Restaurants) to provide cheap but wholesome meals. Food eaten in restaurants was not on ration. By the end of the war there were 2000 British Restaurants serving half a million meals a day. The Ministry of Labour also encouraged, and sometimes forced, employers to provide works canteens. The number of factory canteens increased from 1500 in 1939 to 18 500 by 1945.

These measures marked an important change in the state's attitude to the diet and health of its citizens.

Using the evidence

Lord Woolton was in charge of the Ministry of Food. He was a self-made businessman with a flair for communicating with ordinary people. He became very popular. He realised that publicity and propaganda could play an important part in persuading people to change the eating habits of a lifetime and to try different foods. He used the radio as well as newspapers and magazines to get his message across. The following sources are just a few of the Ministry of Food advertisements that appeared in newspapers during the war years.

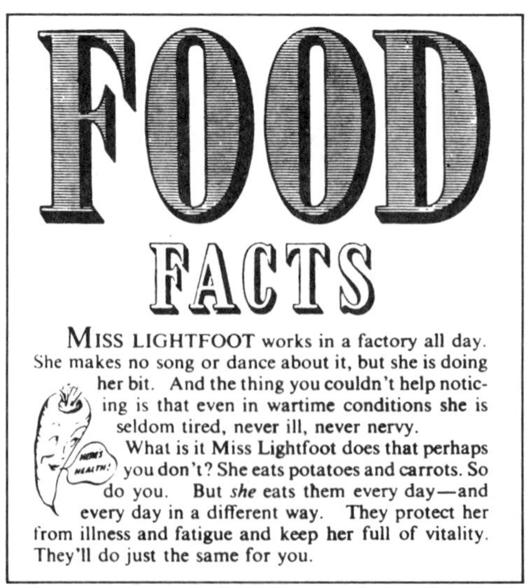

1 List all the different arguments used by the Ministry of Food to persuade people to eat more potatoes and carrots.

2 Which one of these arguments would you have found most convincing? Give reasons for your answer.

3 Successful propaganda is usually based on an element of truth. It then employs a number of different techniques to grab people's attention and influence their opinions and behaviour. The following table shows some of these techniques. Copy the table into your exercise book and then, next to each technique, write an extract from the Ministry of Food advertisements to illustrate it.

Propaganda technique	*Example*
Humour	
Exaggeration and lies	
Appeals to patriotism	
Use of scientific 'facts'	
Appeals to personal vanity	
Appeals to a mother's love for her children	

Which one of these techniques do you find most persuasive? Give reasons for your answer.

Living with rationing

Rationing did not end the shortages, it could only try to ensure that everyone received a share of what was available. As the war continued, shortages became more acute. Indeed, by directing some factories to produce munitions and supplies exclusively for the armed forces, the government actually made the problem worse. Even foods that remained unrationed were often in short supply or of poor quality.

> *[3 June 1941.] Food scarce. I miss the vegetables most.... No tobacco in the shops and cigarettes are a commodity for which one barters. No bitter at the New Inn tonight, I'm told. Queues at the sausage shops but when you've got 'em the sausages are mostly breadcrumbs.... As for razor blades, one simply has to marry a shopkeeper's daughter before one can get hold of a new one.*
>
> George Beardmore: *Civilians at War, Journals 1938–46*, 1984

Tropical fruits virtually disappeared from the shops. Lemons and bananas became great rarities.

I had never saw or eaten a banana. Where I lived there was a prisoner-of-war camp behind us. One day I was walking to the shops when a prisoner called us to the fence and offered us three bananas (for my sister and my brother). Not knowing how to eat it we peeled the banana, ate the skin and threw the inner away.

Six-year-old girl quoted in R. Westall's book, *Children of the Blitz*, 1985

Grapes sold for more than £1 a bunch, and in August 1941 a melon fetched £2 – a small fortune in those days. During 1940 eggs became scarce, as millions of hens had been slaughtered to save feeding stuffs. Even onions were in short supply. Bread remained unrationed until after the war, but the plain white loaf which people preferred virtually disappeared. Instead, housewives were encouraged to buy the 'national wholemeal loaf', which the Ministry of Food introduced in April 1942. This was made from grey, wholemeal flour. People hated it and even the Ministry of Food referred to it as 'this nasty, dirty, dark, coarse, indigestible bread'.

With familiar foods in short supply, people showed great ingenuity in finding substitutes. Favourite dishes were now made with strange new ingredients. Wartime recipes included pea pod soup, beetroot pudding, carrot cookies, hard-time omelette, vinegar cake and prune flan. The versatile potato was used for almost everything. New foods such as whale meat, sheeps' heads, horseflesh, powdered egg and spam were introduced. People were hungry enough to try almost anything once.

Hunger drove people to grow their own food. School playing fields, bomb sites and even grass verges were turned into vegetable patches. Here a London park is turned into a children's 'Victory Garden'. The boy with a butterfly net had a very important job to do. What do you think it was?

blackies: blackbirds

The boys have been out shooting blackies round the corn stacks all day and have got lots. They all eat them in the village here. Johnny says they're very rich. He says sparrows are good, too, but you have to get so many to make a pie.

Thea Tregall quoted in T.H. O'Brien's book, *Civil Defence,* 1955

With so many shortages, all food was precious. The Ministry of Food organised an anti-waste campaign. Wherever people went, on trains and buses as well as in the streets and shops, government posters urged them to shop wisely, to 'make do and mend', to 'dig for victory' and to avoid waste. Penalties for ignoring these warnings could be severe. For example, in February 1941 the assistant master of the Downham Market Institution was fined £5 for wasting 10 lb. 10 oz. of bread.

Government anti-waste posters.

Questions

1 Study the two anti-waste posters.
  a) Explain how wasting food would 'help the Hun'.
  b) Which of these posters do you think was the more effective? Give reasons for your answer.
  c) Design your own anti-waste poster. It must be eye-catching and persuasive.

2 Which of the many shortages described in this chapter would you have found most difficult to accept? Give reasons for your answer.

The effects of rationing

Rationing did not mean that everyone made the same sacrifices. It was not totally fair. For example, many industrial workers in the North and Midlands argued that, because of their heavy manual work, they needed a larger food ration than workers in the South. In addition, the wealthy continued to enjoy certain advantages. They could sometimes find a way of getting foods that were in short supply 'under the counter' or on the 'black market'. Even such rarities as Havana cigars and French wines could be bought at a price. Although penalties for trading on the black market were severe, many people took the risk in order to acquire the occasional luxury.

> *The government posters made us all hate the 'Black Market' – though no one ever knew what a 'Black Marketeer' looked like. But all through the war things kept 'appearing' in our house. One Christmas, a whole unopened box of Mars bars. Another time, a seven pound tin of butter, which for some reason we kept in the bath. . . . When I asked dad where these things came from, he'd say 'bought it off a feller at work' or 'off the ships'.*
>
> Tyneside boy quoted in R. Westall's book, *Children of the Blitz*, 1985

There were also regional variations. Some areas might enjoy plentiful supplies of chocolate, cigarettes or beer, while other areas were virtually without these items. John Rogers discovered this on a day trip from Ipswich to neighbouring Felixstowe:

> *I was amazed at the amount of cakes in the shops – these are 'an event' in Ipswich. There were plenty of chocolates, too; I bought a welcome pound of them.*
>
> Quoted in R. Douglas Brown's book, *East Anglia, 1941*, 1986

But whatever its inequalities, rationing was fairer than simply allowing a free-for-all. It also meant that most people had a more balanced diet than in peacetime. People consumed more vegetables and milk, and less meat, butter and sugar. This had a direct effect on the nation's health. By the end of the war there were fewer people dying from tuberculosis and fewer babies and mothers dying in childbirth than in 1940.

4 AIR-RAID PRECAUTIONS

The Blitz begins

Muriel Gee witnessed the first heavy bombing raids on London on 7 September 1940:

> *One day, in September 1940, I and my close friend from work, Daisy Furlong, went to a colleague's wedding near Herne Hill. During the afternoon we were having drinks in the garden when planes came over. I suppose the sirens went, but I don't remember really – we'd had a few drinks. Anyway, we stood on whatever we could find and watched the explosions as the Germans bombed the docks. We were young, it was happening a few miles away, and we didn't worry.*
>
> *Daisy and I had arranged to go to a cinema in the Old Kent Road that evening, straight from the wedding. We were enjoying the film when a notice came on the screen to say there was an air raid alert and anyone wishing to leave should do so. Well, except for the raid on the docks that afternoon, there had been nothing all these months so we stayed put. After hearing a lot of noise, a while later another notice came on the screen. The raid was heavy, no one was to leave the cinema, but we should all sit under the balcony. This we all did and continued to watch the screen until suddenly, 'whoosh', 'crash', the ceiling began to rain plaster, women screamed and the film stopped. Some people went out, but we stayed and someone started community singing. We were a little apprehensive, but fairly happy. Then more 'whooshing'. A bloke came on stage to say we were all to leave. The bus garage next door had been hit and was burning fiercely. By now we were frightened. Outside, the pavement was covered with broken glass and the sky was glowing red.*
>
> Muriel Gee talking to the author in 1988

This was not the first German raid on the mainland of Britain. Canterbury was bombed as early as the night of 9 May 1940. On 24 May, Middlesbrough became the first industrial town to be attacked, and on 18 June the first bombs fell near London. The German bombing of ports, airfields and aircraft factories intensified in August. This was during the Battle of Britain, when the Luftwaffe attempted to destroy the RAF and gain control of the skies over the English Channel in preparation for a full-scale invasion of Britain. On 15 August Croydon aerodrome was attacked; on the nights of 24 and 30 August and again on the nights of 5 and 6 September the outskirts of London were bombed. This was simply a build up to the

London's burning. Southwark Street in flames.

massive daylight raid on London on 7 September which the Germans intended as a knock-out blow against the capital. On that day 375 German bombers were counted over London, and that night about 250 returned to resume the attack. By dawn the following day 430 Londoners were dead and another 1600 were seriously injured. The London 'Blitz' (from 'blitzkrieg', meaning lightning warfare) had begun. The bombing of London continued for the next 57 nights, with occasional daylight raids as well.

Questions

1 Muriel Gee did not seem particularly frightened by the daylight raid on the London docks. Can you find any clues in her account that could explain her lack of concern?

2 Muriel Gee described the events of 7 September 48 years after they occurred. How reliable is this account as a source of historical evidence? Explain your answer.

3 Look at the photograph of Southwark Street burning. Does it help you to understand the horror of being bombed more vividly than Muriel Gee's account? Explain your answer.

4 The fire shown in the photograph could have occurred at any place, at any time. It might have nothing to do with the London Blitz.
   a) Is there any way of checking when and where this photograph was taken?
   b) Does the photograph itself contain any evidence that it does indeed show a bombed London street?
   c) If there is some doubt as to the exact origin of this photograph, is it useless as historical evidence of the Blitz? Explain your answer.

Beating the Blitz

When the Blitz began most Londoners were as surprised and shaken as Muriel Gee. This was because the previous year had seen very little military action of any kind. People called it the 'bore war'. But although civilians had relaxed, the government and local authorities had not been idle. They had planned and organised a wide range of air-raid defences and had set up civil defence services. Not all of their precautions were later found to be necessary, and some of the predictions made by 'experts' about the effects of aerial bombing proved to be wildly inaccurate.

On the whole, however, British civilians proved to be better prepared and better protected against enemy attack than the Germans. The British Government, sometimes reluctantly, accepted its responsibility for the protection of its citizens. Where its preparations were later found to be inadequate, it was usually ready to adapt and improvise, and where central government proved unable or unwilling to act, local initiative usually found a solution.

Gas!

An official poster of 1939 proclaimed: 'Hitler will give us no warning – so always carry your gas mask.' Gas had been widely used in the trenches in World War I. In 1935 the Italian forces invading Abyssinia had dropped gas bombs on defenceless civilians. By 1939 both Britain and Germany possessed large stockpiles of gas weapons. It seemed likely, therefore, that gas would be used against civilian populations in any future war.

By the outbreak of war, the government had issued everyone in Britain, except for the very young, with a free civilian gas mask – 38 million were issued in all. This compared very favourably with Germany, where even by the end of the war not every civilian had received a gas mask. The standard British civilian gas mask cost only 2s. 6d. to make. It consisted of a rubber face mask with a

Right: *toddlers testing their gas masks.*

Below: *later in the war children aged 2 to $4\frac{1}{2}$ were issued with special 'Donald Duck' and 'Mickey Mouse' masks.*

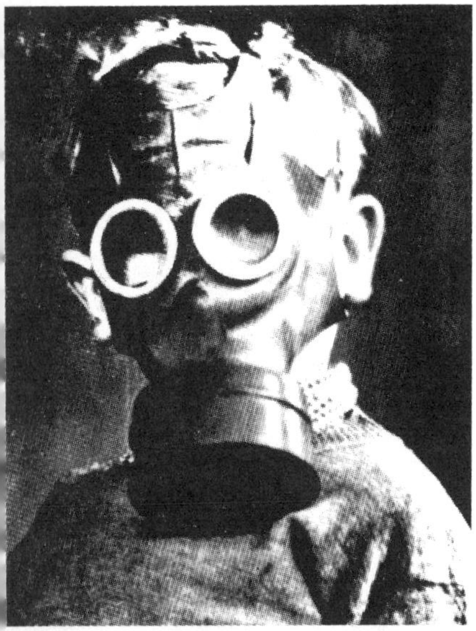

The government provided gas helmets for babies. These were canvas and rubber pods. The mother supplied the air by pumping bellows.

plastic window over the eyes and a small filter at the mouth. Many people found these masks unpleasant to wear.

> *There was a rubber washer under your chin that flipped up and hit you every time you breathed in. You breathed out with a farting noise round your ears. If you blew really hard, you could make a very loud farting noise indeed. (You got caned for doing that during gas practices.) The bottom of the mask soon filled up with spit, and your face got so hot and sweaty you could have screamed.*
>
> Tyneside boy, aged 10, quoted in R. Westall's book, *Children of the Blitz*, 1985

It was never compulsory to carry your gas mask in public, but in the early stages of the war many cinemas and restaurants refused admission to people without their masks. A Mass Observation survey carried out on 6 September 1939 revealed that at least 70 per cent of Londoners were carrying their masks. But as the war went on and no gas bombs fell, most people gave up carrying their masks. Some adapted the containers for carrying more useful items such as sandwiches. The lost property offices at the railway stations were soon stacked high with unclaimed gas masks.

Other anti-gas precautions included coating the tops of pillar boxes with special green or yellow paint that discoloured in the presence of mustard gas, and urging householders to block up cracks in their window frames, door frames and floorboards with putty, as a protection against gas.

In the event, none of these precautions was put to the test. It is possible that the Germans realised that there was little point in using gas weapons against such a well-prepared enemy. More likely, they hesitated to be the first to use a 'terror weapon' that might provoke massive retaliation against their own civilians.

Questions

1 Do you think that the issue of gas masks to all civilians before the declaration of war calmed or alarmed the British public? Give reasons for your answer.

2 Look at the picture of the toddlers testing their gas masks. How can you tell that this photograph was posed for the camera? Do the children look comfortable in their gas masks?

3 Why did the government think it necessary to manufacture special 'Donald Duck' and 'Mickey Mouse' masks for toddlers?

4 Look at the photograph of the baby's anti-gas helmet. Most mothers thought that these helmets were unsafe. Why was this?

5 As gas weapons were never used against civilians in World War II, these expensive precautions were simply a waste of money. Do you agree? Give reasons for your answer.

The blackout

A Public Information Leaflet issued in July 1939 advised that: 'In war, one of our great protections against air attack after nightfall would be the blackout.' The authorities feared that even the faintest glimmer of light after dusk might guide German bombers onto their targets, therefore all public lights were to be put out at night. At first, even smoking in the streets was forbidden. Homes had to be equipped with heavy curtains or shutters at the windows so that no light could escape.

> *We had to prepare blackout curtains or frames with black material nailed to them, to put up at the windows at dusk. Not a chink of light must show, and if it did an air-raid warden would knock and tell you to cover it up. We were also issued with brown sticky tape about $\frac{3}{4}$-inch wide, which we had to put 'criss-cross' across the windows to stop them splintering.*
>
> *All the street lights were put out for the duration and torches had to have their beam covered – only a slit of light was allowed to show. At first cars and buses were allowed no lights at all, but that proved too hazardous, and they were later allowed 'hooded' lights.*
>
> Muriel Gee talking to the author in 1988

Not surprisingly, the early days of the war saw more casualties from the blackout than from enemy action. In January 1940 a Gallup Poll

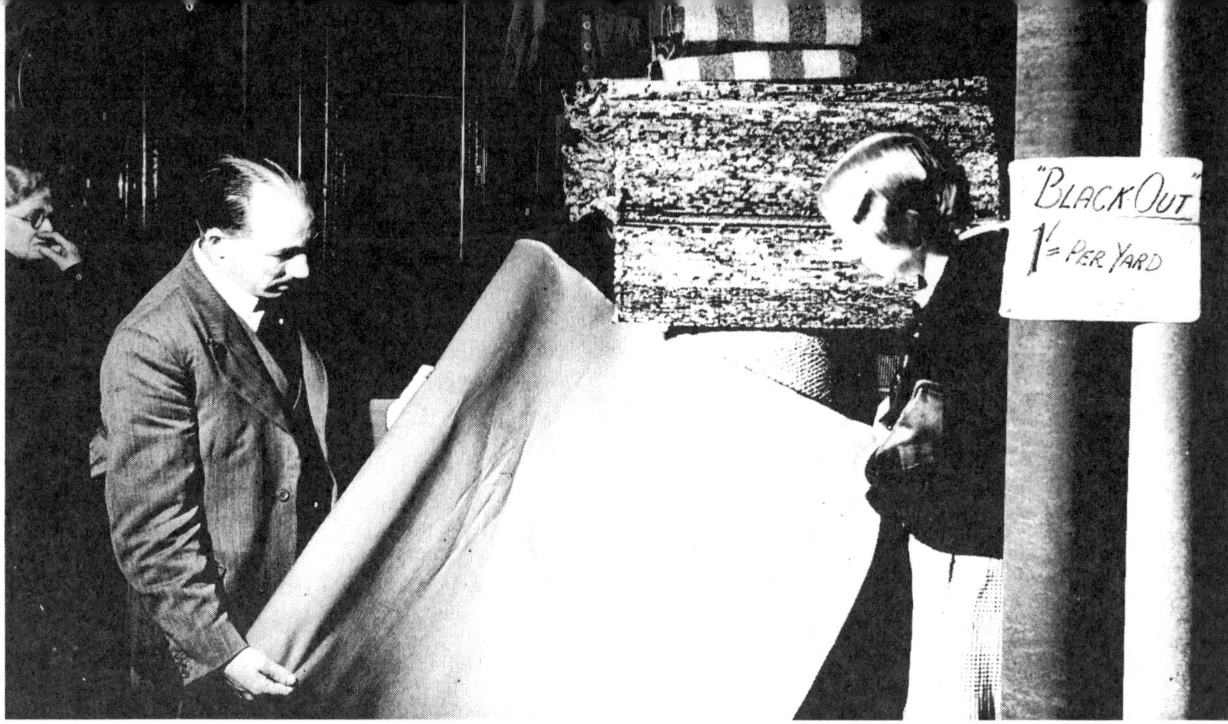

The government arranged for shops to have large stocks of blackout material. However, many shops ran out of supplies in the first rush.

survey revealed that one person in every five claimed to have suffered some sort of injury as a result of the blackout. The trolley buses, which made little noise, were a major hazard. But the casualties were not just from road accidents. Some pedestrians injured themselves walking into lampposts and pillar boxes, while others stumbled into rivers and ponds. To reduce such accidents all stationary street furniture was decorated with generous bands of white paint, and pedestrians tried to make themselves more conspicuous by wearing white clothing or armbands. In May 1941 the government came to the rescue with 'Double Summer Time'. This involved putting the clocks forward by two hours in summer, which provided more hours of daylight at the end of each working day.

The blackout was certainly inconvenient. However, it did provide some of the first and best wartime jokes.

> *One current joke concerned a policeman who shone his torch on a couple in a darkened shop doorway and asked, 'What do you think you're doing in there?' On a nervous male voice answering, 'Er, nothing constable', the policeman was said to have replied, 'Then come out here and hold my torch while I take over!'*
>
> N. Longmate: *How We Lived Then*, 1971

Some town councils did not consider that the blackout offered adequate protection against German bombers and took even more elaborate precautions. The citizens of Sheffield actually erected a dummy town in the neighbouring hills to deceive the Luftwaffe, and the residents of Luton had to burn blocks of sawdust and tar every night to create a thick smokescreen. But despite such efforts, German bombers managed to find their targets with uncanny accuracy.

Servicemen were expected to wear white armbands in the blackout.

Questions

1 Imagine the streets of your town or village totally blacked out. How would this affect your life?

2 What sort of people might have discovered certain advantages in having no street or shop lights?

3 Jokes are designed to make us laugh, not to provide us with useful information. Do you think a historian could extract any useful information from the joke about the blackout? Explain your answer.

Shelters

In the early stages of the war the government backed the idea of small family shelters rather than large public ones. This was because it believed that if a large public shelter was hit by a bomb there would be massive casualties and widespread panic. For similar reasons the government would not allow the Tube stations to be used as shelters. It argued that the underground railway network was needed for the movement of troops and supplies. In fact, the government feared what it called 'deep shelter mentality' – civilians crowding into deep, safe shelters and then refusing to return to the surface to work. When the Blitz began, however, the public simply took the law into their own hands. They bought platform tickets for $1\frac{1}{2}$d. each, and then camped on the station platforms. Although some families did virtually live in the underground system during the Blitz, most people only sheltered there at night. There was no 'deep shelter mentality'. Indeed, the first Shelter Census carried out in London in early November 1940 showed that in the central area of the city only 40 per cent of the inhabitants slept in some sort of shelter. The rest were either working or sleeping in their beds. The government had to accept that its fears of a 'deep shelter mentality' had proved groundless. As a result, in November 1940 it ordered the construction of eight deep and extensive public shelters in London.

In fact the main problem was not how to get people out of the shelters, but how to provide them with essential services while they were in them. The government had not expected people to have to use shelters all night and every night. Consequently, public shelters lacked beds, toilets and canteens. However:

> *All these things were put right in time. The Tubes and the other big shelters were equipped with bunks and a ticket system, with canteens, medical aid posts, and sanitary provision. Indeed, they came to have cinema shows, concert parties, lectures and other communal luxuries.*
>
> *Front Line*, a Ministry of Information pamphlet, 1942

Using the evidence

The following sources provide information about some of the domestic and public air-raid shelters available in World War II.

The Anderson shelter

A *By September 1940, 2 300 000 Andersons had been produced, sufficient to protect 12 500 000 people, nearly a quarter of the population. The Anderson was supplied free to manual workers in danger areas and to others earning under £250 a year.*

N. Longmate: *How We Lived Then*, 1971

B *The very fortunate people at that time who had a garden had what was called an Anderson shelter built in the garden for them. This consisted of a square hole dug in the soil about four feet deep. This was then covered by sheets of corrugated iron. A small entrance was left at one end and the whole construction was then covered with soil and sods of earth.*

Quoted in B. Wicks' book, *No Time to Wave Goodbye*, 1988

C *The Anderson would protect up to six people against practically anything but a direct hit. . . . Many flooded as soon as they were installed. . . . Most of those delivered after the start of the war were . . . somewhat too small to sleep in. . . . They did not shut out the din.*

Angus Calder: *The People's War*, 1969

D

A single German bomb caused this huge crater. The people sheltering in the Anderson shelters in the foreground escaped uninjured. Croydon, August 1940.

Surface brick shelters

E *An unfortunate ambiguity in a Ministry of Home Security circular of the Spring of 1940 persuaded some borough engineers and local builders that these shelters might be constructed without any cement in the mortar at all.... In the London Region alone, well over five thousand shelters were built without cement.... They showed a disconcerting propensity to collapse, through poor construction, when bombs fell near by.*

Angus Calder, as above

a disconcerting propensity: a worrying tendency

F

Brick street shelters being built in Peckham, January 1940.

G One south London woman had this to say about her local shelter:

[It was] so damp and badly built it was not fit to keep hens in, let alone to shelter humanity. After a week of misery, my mother, my brother and myself refused to use it.

Quoted in N. Longmate's book, *How We Lived Then*, 1971

The underground

H *By chance last week I was on the Central Line and saw a mass of people camped out for the night, on the platforms. All very orderly, with helmeted Marshals in charge . . . old people already lying down swathed in blankets, mothers making tea or brewing up soup on camp stoves, and small children watching the train. . . . Some three feet had been left between them and the edge of the platform for the use of passengers.*

George Beardmore: *Civilians at War, Journals 1938–46*, 1984

Central Line: part of the underground railway system

I *The stench was frightful, urine and excrement mixed with strong carbolic, sweat and dirty, unwashed humanity.*

Francis Faviell: *A Chelsea Concerto*, 1959

J *As the train moved out of Bank Station and entered the tunnel, it stopped and all the lights went out. There was a great thud and we held our ears. When we returned we realised a bomb had fallen down the lift shaft of that station and, apart from those killed by the blast, there were also those who had been thrown on the line and electrocuted, just as our train pulled out.*

Bernard Kops: *The World is a Wedding*, 1963

K

In time Tube station platforms were equipped with bunks. Holborn station, January 1941.

Morrison shelters

L *The counter this morning is crowded with applicants for Morrison shelters. These are iron-plated cages with lattice sides, about nine feet by five by four, that one erects inside one's home, preferably in the recess provided by the chimneybreast.... They are intended to be furnished with mattress and pillows and slept in.*

George Beardmore: *Civilians at War, Journals 1938–46*, 1984

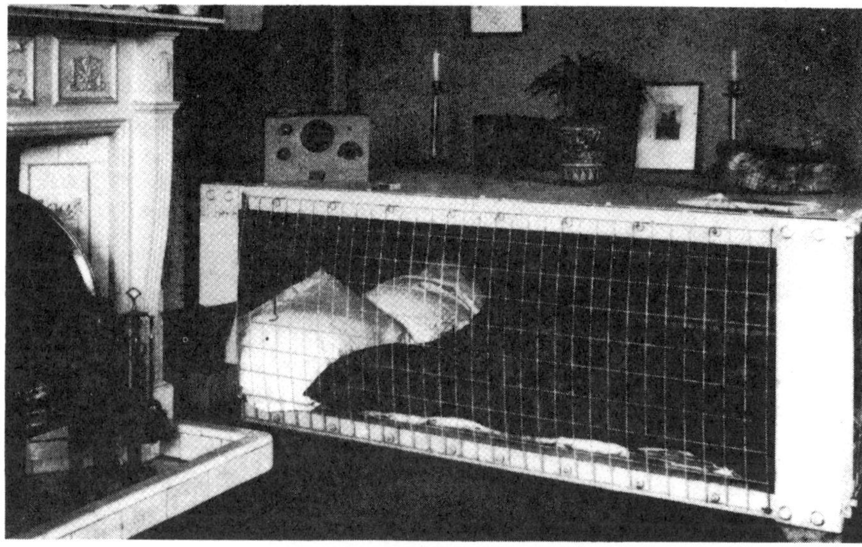

M

A Morrison shelter installed in a living room in 1941. For large families there was a double-decker version. How did this family make extra use of their shelter?

N *Morrisons were supplied free to people earning up to £350 a year and were on sale at about £7 to people earning more.... The Morrison proved the most successful shelter of the war, particularly... when a family had only a few seconds to get under cover.*

N. Longmate: *How We Lived Then*, 1971

1 Award each of these shelters a mark out of 10 (10 = excellent), under the following headings: safety, price, comfort, ease of installation, hygiene, convenience.

2 Which type of shelter would you have chosen? Give reasons for your answer.

3 Some of these sources are primary and others are secondary. Make a list of each.

4 'Primary sources provide first-hand evidence of events. This makes them more reliable than secondary sources.' Argue for or against this statement, using the sources in this section to support your view.

Civil defence

Civil defence was mainly the responsibility of each local authority. In 1937 the Air Raid Precautions Act ordered local authorities to submit their plans for coping with air raids to government inspection. (In September 1941 the original title of Air Raid Precautions – ARP – was officially replaced by the phrase 'civil defence', which now included the fire service as well as the former ARP services.)

The town clerk, or some other senior local government officer, usually became the local ARP controller. His senior officials became the heads of the various services. They worked from a protected control centre linked by telephone to the wardens' posts, ambulance stations, rescue depots, first aid posts, and the other emergency services. The diagram below illustrates the sequence of events that took place when a bomb dropped on a street.

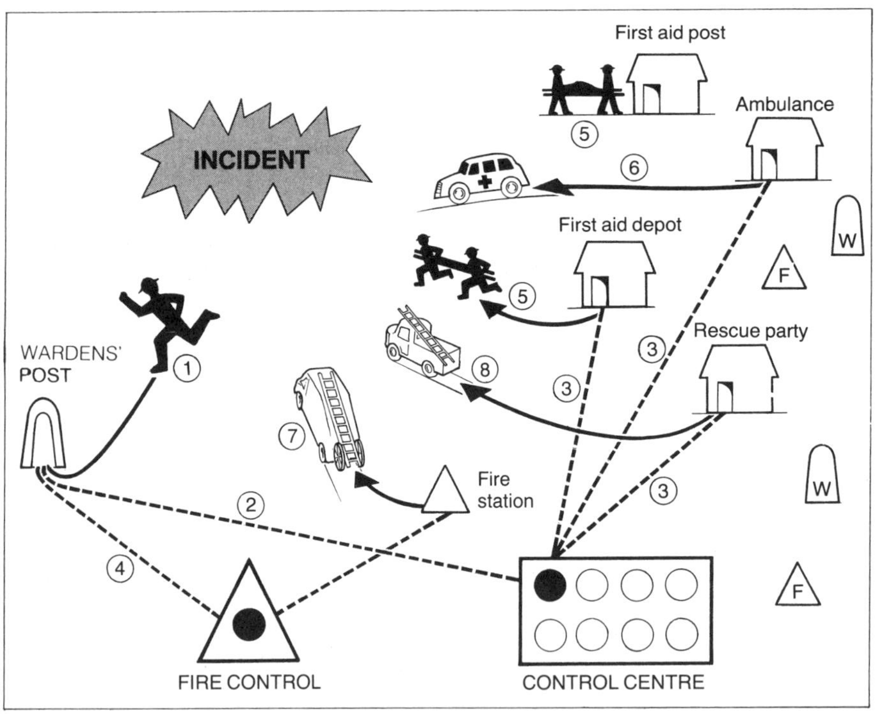

Key

1 A bomb falls. A warden runs to his post to report.
2 The wardens' post informs the control centre.
3 The control centre decides how the incident shall be dealt with and sends out instructions to the services that are needed.
4 The fire brigade receives its call direct from the wardens' post.
5 Stretcher parties leave the first aid posts to deal with minor casualties.
6 Ambulances are sent to collect those who are seriously hurt.
7 Firemen rush to the scene and fight the fires.
8 Rescue men must remove fallen masonry and search for casualties.

If the controller needed reinforcements from other areas, he reported to regional control which then contacted other local control centres and ordered additional services to go to the crisis area.

By December 1940 the civil defence services totalled about one and a half million men and women, of whom about four-fifths were voluntary, part-time members. Civil defence proved an excellent example of local democracy at work. Where the government or local authority failed to see a problem, local people improvised.

While each of the services had a vital role to perform, the wardens and the fire service deserve a particular mention.

Wardens

Most of the wardens were part-timers, and were usually middle-aged or elderly. One in six were women. They were expected to know their local area well, and whether the local residents slept in their beds, under the stairs, or in a garden shelter. An official report written in February 1936 described the wardens' job:

> *Street wardens will be required to act as guide and helper to the general public in the area to which they are allotted. It is particularly important that they should help to prevent panic. . . . They should help to direct people in the streets to the nearest shelter. They should report to the police or the local control centre the fall of bombs, dangerous fires, presence of gas, blocking of roads, damaged mains and any other information that may be required to enable a particular situation to be dealt with.*

This report failed to mention the most unpleasant of the wardens' jobs – having to collect 'unidentified flesh' in a basket after a raid. One warden wrote:

> *We had somehow to form a body for burial so that the relatives (without seeing it) could imagine that their loved one was more or less intact for that purpose. But it was a very difficult task – there were so many pieces missing and, as one of the mortuary attendants said, 'Proper jigsaw puzzle, ain't it, Miss?' The stench was the worst thing about it.*
>
> F. Faviell: *A Chelsea Concerto*, 1959

A warden rescuing a child from a bombed-out building in Buckingham Gate, London, June 1944.

Questions

1 Look again at the official report above, then design a recruiting poster for wardens, including their main duties and responsibilities.

2 What sort of personal qualities and qualifications would you be looking for in candidates for the job of warden?

3 Look at the photograph of a warden rescuing a child.
   a) Was this one of the jobs listed in the 1936 report on wardens?
   b) Has the photographer captured a 'real life' drama here, or was the scene specially posed for him? How do you know?

4 Look back to page 31 and re-read Muriel Gee's account of the blackout. What evidence is there that wardens might not always have been popular figures?

Firemen

If bomb blast caused most injuries, fire caused most damage. The German bombers always dropped a mixture of high explosive and incendiary (fire) bombs. These incendiary bombs were designed to start raging fires in unguarded homes, factories and warehouses. In the two and a half years before the war the number of firemen, fire stations and pumps was increased by ten times. As a result, when the raids first began, four-fifths of London's auxiliary (part-time) firemen had not been in the service long enough to have seen a serious fire. The first fires of the Blitz tested the fire services to the limit. An auxiliary fireman described these early days and nights:

> *Most of us had the wind up to start with. . . . It was all new, but we were all unwilling to show fear, however much we might feel it. . . . The fires had a stunning effect. Wherever the eye could see, vast sheets of flame and a terrific roar. It was so bright that there was no need for headlights.*
>
> *Front Line*, a Ministry of Information pamphlet, 1942

In the first 22 days and nights of the London raids the fire services attended nearly 10 000 fires. These first raids revealed serious faults in the fire services. Reinforcements would arrive at a fire only to discover that their hoses did not fit the local hydrants. Also, they sometimes ran out of water. To solve these problems, the 1666 fire authorities in England and Wales were merged into the National Fire Service in August 1941. In addition, steps were taken to ensure an emergency water supply; massive water tanks were installed at roadsides, in parks and in the cellars of bombed-out buildings. Also in 1941, the government introduced the Fire Guard Scheme, for which

Firemen fighting a blaze in a London street, February 1944.

men aged 16 to 60 were enlisted to serve as fire watchers for several hours each month. From August 1942 the scheme included women aged 20 to 45. It proved equally unpopular with both sexes and as the war dragged on people grew more and more reluctant to turn out at night.

Questions

1 Compare the photograph of a burning London street with the auxiliary fireman's account of his own experiences. What can you learn from the written account that you cannot learn from the photograph?

2 a) Taken as a whole, do you think the government's preparations for coping with the Blitz were adequate?
b) How might they have been improved?

5 COUNTING THE COST

Casualties

Barbara Nixon described the first casualty of the Blitz that she saw:

nauseated: sickened

> *In the middle of the street lay the remains of a baby. It had been blown clean through the window and had burst on striking the roadway. To my intense relief, pitiful and horrible as it was, I was not nauseated, and found a torn piece of curtain in which to wrap it.*
>
> Barbara Nixon: *Raiders Overhead*, 1943

In 1943 a Hull schoolgirl wrote the following letter to the rescue workers who had dug her family out of their bombed home:

> *Just a few lines thanking you for what you did for us on July 14th. . . . How you helped to get my mother out, and to get my two brothers which was dead, how you help to get me to shelter when I hadn't any shoes on my feet.*
>
> Quoted in N. Longmate's book, *How We Lived Then*, 1971

An elderly air-raid warden in Hull described finding his wife in the ruins of their bombed home:

> *She were in the passage between the kitchen and the wash'ouse, where it blowed 'er. She was burnt right up to 'er waist. 'Er legs were just two cinders. And 'er face. The only thing I could recognise 'er by was one of 'er boots – I'd 'ave lost fifteen 'omes if I could 'ave kept my missus.*
>
> From a Mass Observation report on Hull, quoted in A. Calder's book, *The People's War*, 1969

Questions

1 Which of these three accounts describes most vividly the shock and horror of seeing people killed by bombs? Explain your choice.

2 All of these accounts are calm and reasonable. They do not show hatred of the enemy. Try to explain this.

3 What evidence do these three sources provide to show that, in time, ordinary people might have got used to the sight of death and injury?

During World War II, 60 595 civilians were killed by enemy action in Britain; 86 182 were seriously injured, and another 150 833 were slightly injured. Terrible though these figures are, it should be remembered that in Dresden more than 35 000 German civilians were killed in just one British and American bombing raid in 1945.

Civilian casualties in Britain, 1939–45		
The worst-hit towns and cities	*Numbers killed*	*Seriously injured*
Liverpool	2 596	2 148
Glasgow	1 498	1 985
Birmingham	2 319	2 981
Manchester	577	583
Cardiff	345	936
Coventry	1 085	1 895
Hull	1 062	1 017
Southampton	630	898
London	29 890	50 507

Although London suffered nearly 30 000 deaths, its vast size meant that it could survive such casualties. But smaller cities and towns were often stunned and paralysed by their losses. One example was Coventry where on the night of 14 November 1940, in a ten-hour raid, German bombers destroyed 100 acres of the city centre, killing 554 people and seriously injuring another 865. Over the next six months most major British cities and ports became German targets.

On 24 November it was Bristol's turn, and during the following month Birmingham, Southampton, Manchester, Sheffield and Leicester were all bombed. For eight nights at the beginning of May 1941 Liverpool was raided; 1900 people lost their lives and 1450 were seriously injured.

Coventry in ruins.

A V1 'flying bomb' falling on London. When the V1 ran out of fuel, its engine cut out and it crashed to earth. People had only seconds to take shelter.

The climax of these raids came on the night of 10 May with the last and the worst of the big attacks on London. On that one night 1436 people were killed – a record for the war. Thereafter the bombing of British cities became lighter and more sporadic as the Germans redirected their main strength against the Soviet Union. Only in 1944 when the V1 flying bombs and the V2 rockets were launched against London did civilian casualties start to rise again. The V1s killed nearly 6200 people, while the V2s killed a further 2800. These weapons were particularly terrifying because of the speed with which they struck. The V2 could not be heard until it exploded on impact.

In fact, civilian casualty figures were not nearly as bad as the 'experts' and the government had predicted. In 1939 the military expert Basil Liddell-Hart warned that 'nearly a quarter of a million casualties might be expected in the first week of a new war'. The government's own predictions were that each night's bombing would produce at least 3000 deaths, with another 12 000 people seriously injured. One million cardboard coffins were prepared in readiness. Thankfully they were not needed. Over the war as a whole, pre-war estimates of deaths and casualties proved 14 times too high. This was one government miscalculation which no one complained about.

Damage to property

If the government had overestimated the damage to life and limb, it had seriously underestimated the damage to property. By 19 June 1941 more than two million houses had been damaged or destroyed, 60 per cent of them in London. Three years later this figure had

This view of a bombed-out London street gives some idea of the massive damage to property.

risen to about $3\frac{3}{4}$ million – that is, two houses out of every seven. This Plymouth woman's description of her house after a raid was typical of many:

> *No roof. No window panes. The door blasted open. . . . I'd have given my kingdom for a cuppa, but there was no electricity on and no gas. I wasn't to know then that we would be without gas for almost six months.*
>
> Quoted in N. Longmate's book, *How We Lived Then*, 1971

The government failed to foresee the human consequences of the destruction of so many homes. As a result there were inadequate plans for the immediate aftercare of bombed-out families, for emergency food supply and for rehousing the homeless. Rather slowly the government introduced measures to ease the problems. On 28 September 1940 they appointed a Special Regional Commissioner to co-ordinate relief for bombed-out families in London. At the same time several hundred skilled men were released from the Army to reinforce the gas and water mains repair squads; military pioneers were directed to clear wrecked buildings; 25 000 extra labourers were recruited for repair and rebuilding work; and big cranes were brought from the United States and put to work.

Homes that were not completely wrecked were rapidly repaired so that families could return to them. By August 1941 over 1 100 000 damaged houses had been made waterproof and were therefore just about habitable. Even so, many thousands of families remained homeless. They took refuge in the local authority 'rest centres', which were not equipped to shelter and feed large numbers of people for a long period of time. Conditions in some rest centres were squalid. Catering organisations, such as the Londoners' Meal Service,

CITY OF COVENTRY

PREVENTION OF TYPHOID FEVER

In view of present damage to DRAINAGE communications in the City, special precautions against Typhoid Fever are advised:

BOIL ALL DRINKING WATER

This public information poster illustrates one of the problems that resulted from bomb damage. Make a list of other probable problems.

were only slowly set up to provide cheap meals for the homeless. Much of the work was left to voluntary organisations. By and large, central and local government measures to support the homeless were 'too little and too late'.

The effect on industry

There was a real danger that repeated German raids would seriously reduce the output of British industry. In the Coventry raid on 14 November, 21 important factories were severely damaged by fire or a direct hit. In fact, damage was usually quickly repaired and few factories remained out of action for more than a week or two.

Far more worrying was the effect the raids began to have on the output of the British worker. For example, in the early days of the Blitz, workers were spending more time in their shelters than on the factory floor. As a result, on 17 September 1940 Winston Churchill called for the training of some workers as 'lookout men'. They would be stationed on the roofs of factories and office blocks, with instructions to sound an alarm if it seemed that a German aircraft was about to bomb the building. Workers could then crouch under their machines or desks for protection. This saved repeated visits to shelters and, as the system was slowly adopted, production rose again.

A further worry was that workers who had spent sleepless nights in shelters, and had perhaps been bombed out of their homes, would fail to turn up for work in the morning. In fact, during the winter of 1940–41 absenteeism from work in most firms was actually less than usual. Mark Benney, a worker in an aircraft factory, explained:

> *There was little absenteeism caused by the raids, in part because we all felt that the raids gave an added importance to our work, but much more because we knew that if we didn't turn up our mates would be worrying.*
>
> M. Benney: *Over to Bombers*, 1943

Finally, there was the real possibility that the German raids would so damage communications that people would be unable to get to work even if they wanted to. Certainly after very heavy raids this sometimes proved to be the case. But people were usually so anxious to get into work that they put up with lengthy detours and used unusual methods of transport to get there. An office girl from Tooting in south London described the difficulty she had trying to get to work in the City on Monday, 9 September 1940:

> *The Tube was closed at Balham. I hitch-hiked a lift from a lorry driver who took me to Elephant and Castle and from there I walked to the City. We walked over Southwark Bridge as we were not allowed to cross London Bridge. . . . Rubble and glass were all over*

Getting to work in London the morning after a raid.

the place, and there was a gas main belching flames at the end of the bridge.

Quoted in N. Longmate's book, *How We Lived Then*, 1971

Thanks to determination like this, the Germans failed to disrupt British industry too seriously.

Questions

1 Do you think the lookout men on factory and office roofs offered any real protection from German bombs? Explain your answer.

2 Why was it so important for Britain that civilians continued to get to work every morning, even after heavy raids?

3 Why, according to Mark Benney, were people more determined than ever to turn up for work during the Blitz? Try to think of other reasons, as well.

Using the evidence: the effect on morale

The German raids on British cities were meant to destroy essential services, terrify the civilian population and break their will to continue the war. Mass panic and hysteria would force the British Government to ask for peace. Of course, Britain did not surrender. There was no widespread panic. Or was there? Examine the following sources to find an answer to this question.

phlegm: coolness

A *The legend of British self-control and phlegm is being destroyed. All reports from London agree in stating that the population is seized by fear – hair-raising fear. The 7 000 000 Londoners have completely lost their self-control. They run aimlessly about in the streets and are the victims of bombs and bursting shells.*

Broadcast on German-controlled French radio, 18 September 1940

B *My latest reports are that there is no sign of panic anywhere in the East End. . . . The inhabitants are shaken by continued lack of sleep but no sign of panic and no wish to evacuate. No defeatist talk.*

Telegraphic report by the Metropolitan Commissioner of Police, 12 September 1940

C *Women were seen to cry, to scream, to tremble all over, to faint in the street, to attack firemen and so on. . . . There were several signs of suppressed panic as darkness approached.*

Mass Observation report on the Coventry raid of 14 November 1940

D *Everyone who can do so is leaving the town. . . . For the time morale has collapsed. I went from parish to parish and everywhere there was fear.*

The Bishop of Winchester describing Southampton after a heavy raid on 2 December 1940. Quoted in A. Calder's book, *The People's War*, 1969

E *The German attack upon London has had no fundamental ill-effect either upon the capital or upon the nation. . . . Nothing has affected the unconquerable optimism of the Cockney.*

A report from the Home Security Operations Rooms, 25 September 1940

F *I see the damage done by the enemy attacks; but I also see, side by side with the devastation and amid the ruins, quiet, confident, bright and smiling eyes, beaming with a consciousness of being associated with a cause far higher and wider than human or personal issues. I see the spirit of an unconquerable people.*

Winston Churchill, 12 April 1941

G
Punch cartoon, May 1941

1 Make one list of the sources that claim civilian morale was good, and another list of the sources that suggest panic.

2 Examine the sources that claim there was fear and confusion after heavy German raids. Which of these sources do you trust and which do you mistrust? Explain your choice.

3 a) Make a list of the sources that are clearly propaganda – that is, sources that are trying to change people's opinions and are not just reports of what happened.
b) Are these propaganda sources of any value to a historian investigating the effects of the Blitz on civilian morale? Explain your answer.

4 a) The *Punch* cartoon (source **G**) is not an entirely flattering view of the British national character. It suggests a certain amount of stupidity. Explain how it suggests this.
b) Do you think this cartoon would have boosted or undermined people's morale? Discuss your views with the rest of the class.

5 On balance do you think the German raids caused widespread panic and hysteria? Use the sources in this chapter to support your answer.

6 WOMEN AT WAR

Using the evidence

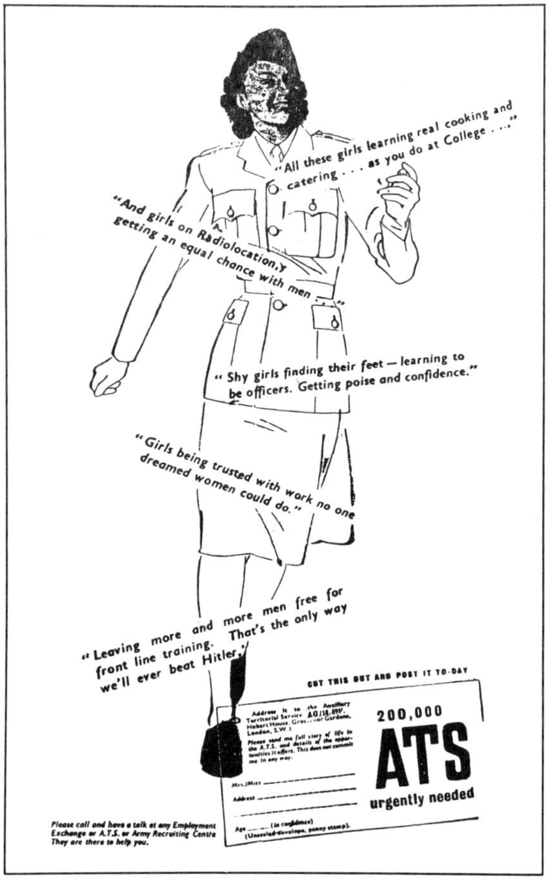

A *Cambridge Daily News, 10 October 1941.*

B *Cambridge Daily News, 16 October 1941.*

C APPEAL TO THE WOMEN OF CAMBRIDGE.
THEIR PLACE IN WAR WORK.

Sir Will Spens's Message.

The ever-widening fighting front, with its relentless drain upon manpower and materials, has made it clear beyond all doubt that we cannot win this war against Hitlerism without the united backing of our entire resources. . . .

I appeal to every woman who can come forward now and offer her services either in one of the women's auxiliary services or for factory work. . . . Every woman volunteer enables the Government to release a man for duties which only a man can fulfil.

Cambridge Daily News, 4 October 1941

1 What, according to all three sources, was the main reason for directing women into factories and the Forces?

2 Sources A and B use very different techniques to persuade women to 'do their bit'. Make a list of all the ways in which these two sources differ.

3 Which of the advertisements (sources A and B) would have been more likely to persuade you to do something for the war effort? Explain your answer.

4 a) Which of the three sources suggests that women might actually gain something personally from their war work?
b) What might they gain?

5 What evidence is there in these three sources to suggest that women were not considered capable of doing exactly the same work as men even in wartime?

Registration and conscription of women

By 1941 the government was anxious to mobilise women for the war effort. With so many men in the Forces, industry was suffering a labour shortage. With more women in factories, yet more men would be available for military service. This was a lesson that had been learnt and applied in World War I.

Ironically, the opening years of World War II actually saw an increase in women's unemployment. This was because many of the industries women had always worked in, such as textiles and clothing, cut back their workforces when the war began. At first women found it difficult to get other jobs. Even by January 1941 there were 350 000 women registered as unemployed.

In March 1941 the government finally acted. It ordered all women aged 19 to 40 to register at employment exchanges. The Ministry of Labour compiled a record of what they were doing and could direct suitable women into 'essential work'. Housewives who could prove that they were fully occupied at home, and mothers caring for children under 14, were not forced into war work. But single women without anyone to support were directed to work wherever they were needed, even if it meant living away from home.

Compulsory registration was followed by the National Service Number 2 Act, introduced in December 1941. This meant that single women between 20 and 30 could be called up for military service. The Act proved necessary because of the reluctance of many women to volunteer for the Forces.

By the end of 1941 Britain had done more than any other country to mobilise its entire population for war. Whole sectors of industry were virtually taken over by women. There were 300 000 women working in explosives and chemicals, and more than 1 500 000 women working in the engineering and metal industries. In lighter engineering, women sometimes made up 80 per cent of the entire workforce. In addition, there were 500 000 women in civil defence and more than 450 000 women in the Forces. By 1943 it was estimated that at least 7 750 000 women were in paid work.

D (above): *Women workers at a tank factory in the north-east of England, March 1942.*

Using the evidence

The government was anxious to prove that women were committed to the war effort. Propaganda showed them eagerly and patriotically working for the defeat of Nazi Germany. Official photographs usually featured attractive young women, often in uniform, happily and confidently taking on new responsibilities. Meanwhile, government ministers and the press showered women with extravagant praise, not only for taking on unfamiliar roles, but also for working as effectively as men.

This was only one side of the story, however. Some people suggested that not all women were enthusiastic about their new jobs or the war effort. In 1943 Mass Observation investigated a small factory in Wiltshire. The researcher reported 'aimlessness, irresponsibility and boredom' amongst the female workers. Other sources also suggested that women thoroughly disliked their often tedious work and were looking forward to the day when they could give it up.

A *The work the women are performing in munition factories has to be seen to be believed. Precision engineering jobs which a few years ago would have made a skilled turner's hair stand on end are performed with dead accuracy by girls who had no industrial experience.*

Clement Attlee, Churchill's deputy, September 1942

B *...the greatest amount of absenteeism is among the younger women without ties. Their 'don't care' attitude causes welfare officers a lot of problems....Young and self-centred, and probably pampered at home, they want factories merely as shelters.*

They say about different jobs, 'Oh, I can't do this' or 'I can't do that' and want moving to some other job which they think might be easier or cleaner. They lack the real war spirit.

Daily Mirror, 5 February 1942

C *The day the war is over I'll be the first one out of here. I'll be down that path before they've finished announcing it.*

A factory girl quoted in 'War Factory', a Mass Observation survey, 1943

E (above): *'Ruby Loftus screwing a breech-ring.' A painting by Dame Laura Knight.*

F (left): *The original caption to this photograph read: 'Another party of sales girls left London to take up work in a munition factory in the north of England. The girls are eager to start their new wartime job.' January 1942.*

G *Of all types of temporary labour we employed during the war, the land girls were the best. They soon became accustomed to the work and did not mind what job it was. . . . They were of course excellent with animals.*

A Surrey farmer quoted in N. Longmate's book, *How We Lived Then*, 1971

H *A land girl helping with the harvest, 1944.*

I *Women spreading manure.*

J *A land girl driving a tractor.*

K *Women planting potatoes.*

L The Women of Britain: A Tribute.

Said H.M. Major, news editor of 'La Press', published in Montreal: 'It is the women of Britain who particularly stand out in this war. We have seen women of the Red Cross, the Services and Civil Defence. We have seen them working huge and complicated machines in the factories and stooping to mend the roads with a pick and shovel and we find them – magnificent. I cannot praise your women too much.'

Daily Mail, October 1942

M *An ATS (Auxiliary Territorial Service) girl driving an army lorry, January 1941.*

N *Women ambulance drivers waiting for orders outside a Chelsea garage.*

1 Using all of these sources, make a list of the different types of war work done by women. Underline those jobs which women had probably not done before the war.

2 Examine the picture sources.
   a) Divide a page of your exercise book into two columns. On one side make a note of the pictures you think are natural and realistic. On the other side list the pictures which show women's war work in a glamorous and romantic light (propaganda).
   b) In what ways are all the propaganda pictures similar?
   c) Propaganda is the art of persuasion. It gives the reader or viewer a particular version of events. What impression of women at war do the propaganda pictures leave you with?
   d) In what ways do the more realistic pictures create a different image of women at war?
   e) Source **E** is actually a painting. All the other picture sources are photographs. Does it necessarily follow that the painting is a less reliable piece of evidence on women at war than the photographs? Explain your answer.

3 Examine the written sources. Some of these state that women worked with skill and dedication. Others imply that women disliked their work and were sometimes lazy.
   a) Is it possible that *all* of these sources are, in fact, telling the truth? Explain your answer.
   b) What other types of evidence might you consult before making up your mind on this issue? Discuss this question with the rest of the class.

Continuity and change

Many women gained a great deal of personal satisfaction from their war work. They made new and lasting friendships, enjoyed new-found independence, and discovered new abilities and skills. But in only a few areas did women achieve any permanent improvement to their lifestyle and social status. Overall, there was more continuity than change.

Employment

World War II certainly increased the number of women at work. To a certain extent this trend continued after the war. Even in 1951 women still made up 22 per cent of the engineering workforce, compared with just 10 per cent in 1939. But it would be wrong to explain this increase in female employment just in terms of the effects of war. Even before World War I nearly 5 500 000 women had been in paid employment. In the 1920s and '30s this figure had been steadily rising. As early as 1935, one in three workers in the electrical engineering industry was a woman. It has been estimated that if this peacetime trend had continued, about 6 750 000 women would have been in paid employment by 1943. As we have seen, the actual figure was about 7 750 000, which means that an extra 1 000 000 women were probably working as a direct result of the war. Although this is a significant number, it does not amount to a revolution in patterns of female employment.

There was, however, a significant change in the number of married women at work. Before the war it had been usual for women teachers and civil servants to resign their posts on marriage. The war changed that. By 1943 nearly 3 000 000 widows and married women were employed. Two years later nearly eight out of every ten married women had full-time jobs, while many others managed to do part-time work. By 1945 it was generally accepted that married women who wanted or needed to go out to work could do so.

Pay

With more women joining trade unions in the war years, there was an increase in women's wages. Women's average weekly earnings rose from £1 12s. 6d. (£1 62½p) to £3 3s. 2d. (£3 16p) between October 1938 and July 1945. But the gap between men's and women's earnings hardly changed at all. In January 1944 women in metalwork and engineering earned on average £3 10s. 0d. (£3 50p) a week, whereas the men earned £7 0s. 0d. By 1945 women still earned only 52 per cent of men's earnings.

Male attitudes

Most men saw the increased employment of women during the war as only a temporary measure. They feared the impact that an influx of women would have on their wages and status. Shop stewards warned that some bosses might keep women on at the end of the war, as a source of cheap and 'docile' labour. Male unemployment would then increase. Hardly surprisingly, many men regarded female workers with a mixture of suspicion and hostility.

Mark Benney described the contempt with which he and his workmates in an aircraft factory greeted the arrival of the first woman worker in 1942:

> *We watched the dainty way she picked up a file, with red enamelled fingertips extended as though she were holding a cup of tea. We watched the way she brushed the filings off her overalls after every few strokes, the awkward way she opened and closed her vice, her concern for the cleanliness of her hands, her delicate unhandy way with a hammer.*
>
> M. Benney: *Over to Bombers*, 1943

This Punch *cartoon published in May 1941 reflects the widely held view that women would not be able to cope with engines or machines.*

In time, the obvious competence of many women workers won the grudging respect of men. But this only increased male fears that women would take over their jobs at the end of the war. In 1945 men campaigned through their trade unions to get women out of the factories and back to their homes.

The double burden

In some respects the war actually increased the drudgery and misery of many women's lives. Although mothers of young children were not forced to work, they were encouraged to find some sort of employment. However, they were still expected to manage all their household chores as well. Indeed, far from reducing the traditional pressures on women, the government sometimes increased them, for example by urging women to 'make do and mend'.

It is hardly surprising that women's sickness rate was half as much again as that of men, or that women's absenteeism was double that of men. Many women simply could not cope with the double burden of running a home and working in a factory. A Birmingham woman complained:

> *I'm going home to do an evening's scrubbing. First I've got to do my bit of shopping on the way home. I have to queue for it, because they make no allowances for me being in the factory all day. My two little boys are in school all day. They have their dinners there, and the teacher keeps them until 6 o'clock when I call for them. But I have to get a meal ready, and there's always some washing and mending to do every night.*
>
> Mass Observation survey, quoted in G. Braybon and P. Summerfield's book, *Out of the Cage*, 1987

The government did do something to help working mothers with young children by increasing the number of day nurseries from just 14 in October 1940 to 1500 by 1944. Even so, there were places for only a quarter of all the children under five whose mothers were doing war work. Most mothers had to sort out their own problems by finding 'minders' or baby sitters.

Class differences

Inevitably, women from different social backgrounds were thrown together for the first time in the factories or in the Forces. For some women this was an education in itself and helped to dispel long-held prejudices. Aline Whalley, the daughter of a bank manager, described her surprise at discovering that working-class women were just like her:

> *The war really did a lot of good to girls like me who had been privately educated, it really did. It taught me that working-class people could have emotions, and that they could be bright, really*

Women with toddlers demonstrating for more nurseries.

bright, because my goodness some of those girls were clever. These were things I had simply never considered before.

Quoted in G. Braybon and P. Summerfield's book, *Out of the Cage*, 1987

But such experiences were rare. On the whole, the mobilisation of women simply reinforced the old class divisions. For example, relatively few educated middle-class women went into factories. Most of them opted for the more glamorous Forces, with the WRNS being the most exclusive and the ATS the least popular. Within the Forces it was usual for the working-class recruits to do the manual work, while the middle-class recruits were given the more interesting administrative and secretarial jobs. In addition, middle-class women were often better prepared for life away from home by their experiences at boarding school. This inequality was even more evident among the working women who had young children – middle-class women could usually afford to employ nannies and home-helps to reduce their domestic burden. In these ways, most middle-class women had a far easier war than their working-class sisters.

New sexual attitudes

War work certainly gave many women more money in their purses and more freedom from the watchful eyes of fathers and husbands. Working women learnt more about the world around them and sometimes experimented with new lifestyles. Inevitably, the war offered women new opportunities for casual relationships with men. Some people claimed that women became more promiscuous as a result.

Sexual morality has decayed a great deal in recent years.... Promiscuity is no longer considered wicked....No one seems to see any value in fidelity to one and the same partner.

Views of a male clerk in his 30s, quoted in a Mass Observation survey, 1945

This view received some support from the massive wartime increase in reported cases of venereal disease, in the number of illegitimate births and in the divorce rate. Many women now demanded the same sexual freedom as men. They also expected more from their relationships and were less ready to tolerate unhappy marriages. This set the pattern for many post-war marriages which were based on a more equal and companionable relationship than before.

Women's self-image

The most important change that came about as a result of women's war work was in the way women saw themselves. Women who had experienced new challenges and opportunities would not meekly return to their kitchens.

> *I thought of stacks of dirty crocks to tackle after tea, of pictures and furniture that were once polished every week, and now got done when I had the time. I wondered if people would* ever *go back to the old ways. I cannot see women settling to trivial ways – women who have done worthwhile things.*
>
> Nella Last, a Barrow housewife, writing in her diary on 5 December 1942. Quoted in G. Braybon and P. Summerfield's book, *Out of the Cage*, 1987

As Zelma Katin, a 'clippie' on the Sheffield buses, wrote: 'We all wanted more interesting lives than we used to lead.' The war increased women's expectations and their awareness of their own worth. They became less tolerant of continuing inequalities and exploitation. Women discovered a new pride, self-confidence and purpose.

Questions

> *After 1945 what was important in life was still emphatically male, whether one was looking at work, leisure, politics, language or for that matter the way that historical accounts were written.*
>
> G. Braybon and P. Summerfield: *Out of the Cage*, 1987

1 What evidence in this chapter supports the view that men and male attitudes continued to dominate British society at the end of World War II?

2 a) Make a list of the ways in which women's lives were changed as a result of their wartime experiences.
b) Which one of these changes do you think was most important to women at that time? Explain your choice.
c) Which one of these changes was most important for its long-term effect on the lives of women? Explain your answer.

3 Change does not always mean progress. Write down the ways in which women's lives were made more difficult as a result of the war.

4 Braybon and Summerfield claim that even the way the history of World War II is written is unfair to women. Too often the emphasis is placed on the contribution of men, and women are ignored. Do you think that this book is guilty of underestimating the role of women in World War II? Give reasons for your answer.

7

THE HOME GUARD

On Tuesday, 14 May 1940, Anthony Eden, the new Secretary of State for War, made a radio broadcast to the nation. He wanted men to join a new force of Local Defence Volunteers (LDV).

We want large numbers of...men in Great Britain, who are British subjects between the ages of seventeen and sixty-five...to come forward now and offer their services....The name of the new force which is now to be raised will be 'The Local Defence Volunteers'.... This is...a part-time job....You will not be paid, but you will receive a uniform and will be armed.

Quoted in N. Longmate's book, *The Real Dad's Army*, 1974

By this time the 'bore war' was over and the fighting had started in earnest. The British Expeditionary Force was helping to defend Norway, Belgium, Luxembourg and France against the advancing German armies. Holland surrendered to the Germans the very day of Eden's appeal. With British forces committed in Europe, the original purpose of the LDV (renamed the Home Guard in July 1940) was to be on the lookout for spies and saboteurs, and to guard against surprise German parachute attacks on Britain. As the news from France worsened, the role of the LDV was expanded.

By 24 May the British Expeditionary Force was virtually surrounded by the Germans and had to be evacuated from Dunkirk. It left most of its heavy equipment on the beaches. Four weeks later France surrendered. Britain now stood alone and faced the very real threat of a German invasion. Eastern England was defended by just six infantry divisions at less than half their normal strength. There was a shortage of machine guns, fewer than half the normal number of field guns and only a handful of anti-tank guns. Hired civilian coaches were the troops' only transport. The Local Defence Volunteers were now called upon to strengthen these pitiful defences.

The response

Eden's appeal brought an instant response. By the end of the first day a quarter of a million men had enrolled. The crush of volunteers at a police station in Birmingham was typical:

Applicants seemed to form a never-ending stream. They started to queue up as soon as they could leave their work and by 11 p.m. there were still scores of them wanting to enrol....Within a few days the platoon was three to four hundred strong.

An ex-police officer, Canterbury Road Police Station, quoted in N. Longmate's book, as above

By the end of June the LDV numbered one and a half million men.

Volunteers rush to join the Defence Corps in Cambridge, May 1940.

The volunteers came from all walks of life and all parts of the country. Some were only 15 or 16 years old, while others were well over the upper age limit of 65.

> *There were shepherds, farm hands, gardeners, village shopkeepers, a retired civil servant from India, a retired school master, and one or two folk who worked in London and had cottages in downland.*
>
> T. Wintringham: *New Ways of War*, 1940

This was a people's army. Military ranks and commissions were not introduced until February 1941. In its early days the LDV had a strong democratic spirit. At Hauxton, south of Cambridge, the 29 members of the village LDV met in a schoolroom and elected their own commander from three candidates. In other parts of the country retired army officers and veterans from World War I offered themselves as suitable commanders. Slowly, military discipline emerged from a mixture of government direction and local improvisation.

One pressing question remained. The men were there; the enthusiasm was certainly there. But could the LDV operate as a fighting force?

Questions

1 What evidence is there in Eden's radio broadcast that the government intended the LDV to be an inexpensive force?

2 What can you learn from the photograph of men queuing to join the LDV in Cambridge about the different types of people who volunteered? Does it prove the claim that men of all ages and from a variety of backgrounds came forward?

A fine body of men

Fitness

The only official statement on the volunteers' physical condition was that they 'must be capable of free movement'. This was hardly a severe test of fitness. As a result many of the early recruits were middle-aged, overweight, short-sighted and sometimes even infirm. Elderly, flabby, bespectacled Home Guardsmen were an obvious target for jokes. The historian of the 2nd Isle of Ely Home Guard Battalion recorded the case of a short-sighted Home Guardsman who wandered into a field where a bull was on the loose. As the bull attacked him he grasped its horns and attempted to throw it. Finally the bull ran off. The Guardsman returned to his platoon commander, who commended him for his extraordinary courage.

> *Still panting and mopping his brow, the short-sighted Guardsman replied, 'Oh, but if only I could have stuck to him a few minutes more I'd have had the b—— off his bike.'*
>
> *We Also Served*, the story of the Home Guard in Cambridgeshire and the Isle of Ely, 1940–43, compiled by the Territorial Army Association, 1944

But after the first rush of volunteers, when virtually everyone was accepted, standards were raised. The senile and seriously unfit were weeded out. The situation was improved still further in 1942 with the introduction of 'compulsion'. This meant that men aged 18 to 51 could be 'directed' to join the Home Guard and had to do up to 48 hours' training or guard duties a month. By the summer of 1943 the average age of the Home Guard was under 30.

An elderly clergyman receiving instruction in rifle drill.

Uniform

Eden had promised every volunteer a uniform and a weapon, but he had not said how long it would take to deliver them. As the LDV

Below left: *inspection of LDV unit 'in full uniform' in a London park.*

was formed in rather a hurry, the government had not had time to organise vital supplies and equipment. Consequently, the LDV's first uniforms were simply armbands (called brassards) with the letters 'LDV' (later 'HG') stencilled on them.

By August 1940 most units were receiving their first supplies of army 'denims'. Forage hats followed later. The uniforms and hats were issued without any reference to the men who had to wear them, with inevitable consequences:

> *The issue of clothing (denims) was arduous but had its lighter side. At Ely issues were made throughout the night, and the next day there was a plaintive message from Whittlesey offering small sizes in exchange for large. At the same time a platoon commander wrote to complain that the caps were too small for his men. Getting no reply and fearing that he had given offence he cancelled the letter and wired that his men were too big for the caps.*
>
> *We Also Served*, as above

One Ely unit looked so ridiculous in their ill-fitting uniforms that a local comedian quipped:

> *It won't matter now if Hitler does come, for when he sees this lot he'll just die o' laughing.*
>
> *We Also Served*, as above

In September 1940 boots, greatcoats and cap badges were issued and a month later the Home Guard received their first proper army battledress suits. However, it was almost another eight months before they were fully equipped with ammunition pouches, packs and gaiters. A year after Eden's broadcast, the Home Guard at last began to look like soldiers.

Below: *volunteers on parade with broomsticks instead of rifles, June 1940.*

Weapons

No doubt the volunteers could have fought without uniforms, but there was nothing they could do without weapons. In the days immediately after Dunkirk, every serviceable weapon was needed for the regular army. In any event, the government was in no great hurry to arm a citizen army largely made up of the lower classes. In Berkshire one battalion received, as its first issue of weapons, just four rifles per 100 men and only 10 rounds of ammunition per rifle. In these circumstances the volunteers had to improvise. Sportsmen supplied their own shotguns or sporting rifles, while others manufactured a variety of medieval weapons, from coshes to pikes.

> *My earliest memory is that of detailing men for guard duty in May 1940, and in the absence of anything more lethal, handing them packets of pepper, short lengths of lead cabling and iron tubing.*
>
> A company commander in the 6th Cambridge Battalion, quoted in *We Also Served*, as above

A Sussex unit designed a crossbow for firing grenades, while a Durham unit produced a home-made flame thrower. However, the most popular 'do-it-yourself' weapon was the Molotov cocktail – a bottle filled with petrol and plugged with a petrol-soaked rag. This was for setting enemy tanks on fire. Not surprisingly, such weapons inflicted more casualties on the Home Guard than on the Germans.

> *On one occasion a platoon commander had just thrown one of these missiles [a Molotov cocktail] and was explaining to his men that they were foolproof. . .[when] Private Buggins stepped forward from the ranks, halted three paces from the platoon commander and saluted smartly. 'Yes Buggins.' 'Excuse me, sir, your breeches are on fire.'*
>
> The historian of the 1st Isle of Ely Home Guard Battalion, writing in *We Also Served*, as above

In July 1940 the situation was slightly improved by the arrival of a large shipment of World War I vintage rifles from the United States. However, it was 1942 before every Home Guardsman was issued with a rifle and 1943 before units were equipped with mortars and small field guns. Only when the threat of invasion was long past did the Home Guard have the means to resist it.

Question

Copy out the chart below. Using the sources and information in this section,.identify the main weaknesses of the Home Guard in the first few months of its existence. Next to each weakness write a few notes about how important it would have been if the Germans had invaded. Finally, in the third column, explain how and when these weaknesses were overcome.

Weaknesses	*Importance*	*Remedies*

Using the evidence

The popular image of the Home Guard today is that of 'Dad's Army' – a disorganised and rather comic collection of elderly gentlemen and feeble-minded boys playing at soldiers. Even during the war the Home Guard was often viewed as a joke. But opinions differed then, as now, on the usefulness of the Home Guard. Was it simply a way of distracting people from the very real dangers facing Britain in 1940? Was it a waste of valuable resources? Could it have done anything to repulse a German invasion? The following sources provide conflicting answers.

A *I have also joined the Local Defence Volunteers.... We drill in the Concert Hall with broomsticks, have inspections in which the same unlucky fellow with long hair is repeatedly told to visit the barber's, and are likely to serve no useful purpose whatever should Germans appear in Upper Regent Street.*

George Beardmore: *Civilians at War, Journals 1938–46*, 1984

B *[The Home Guard was] probably doing more harm than good. It tied up production that could have made life a little easier for the hard-pressed civilian, and deprived men now working flat-out for the war effort of precious sleep and recreation.*

N. Longmate: *The Real Dad's Army*, 1974

C
Punch *cartoon, July 1941.*

"Halt! Who goes there?"

D *Such a force is of the highest value and importance. A country where every street and every village bristles with resolute, armed men is a country which... would not be able to be overthrown.*

Winston Churchill, Prime Minister, November 1940

E *As a means of taking over the duties of guarding important sites we were very useful, as many thousands of regular troops were released for more important duties. As rear duty troops in an invasion we would have been useful, but not as front-line combat troops.*

James Frewin, 'A' Company, 4th Battalion Middlesex Home Guard. Quoted in Alastair and Anne Pike's book, *The Home Front in Britain*, 1985

F *History may laugh at us, as we certainly have laughed at ourselves; but does it matter?. . . . We of the Home Guard know full well that in 1940 and 1941 we were the biggest bluff ever, and Hitler dared not call it.*

The historian of the 2nd Cambridge and Suffolk Home Guard Battalion, writing in *We Also Served*, 1944

G *Volunteers intended to defend their villages and streets, and to blow up a few tanks in the process. As equipment, very slowly, became available, Britain acquired a network of amateur garrisons which would have harassed and held up a determined invader.*

Angus Calder: *The People's War, Britain 1939–45*, 1969

H
A Punch *cartoon by Giles.*

" I want you men to imagine the enemy are approaching in large numbers, supported by tanks, flamethrowers, paratroops, etc., etc. . . ."

1 Winston Churchill had overall responsibility for managing the British war effort. Does this mean that his comments (source **D** on the Home Guard must be more reliable than the others? Explain your answer.

2 Which one of these sources do you think provides the most balanced assessment of the Home Guard? Explain your choice.

3 Divide a page of your exercise book in half. On one side write down all the arguments in favour of the Home Guard and on the other side list the arguments against it.

4 What are your conclusions on the usefulness of the Home Guard?

The Home Guard manning an anti-aircraft gun.

The Home Guard with defused bombs.

They also served...

The Home Guard was never put to the test by a German invasion, but it did perform a number of vital services. At first, its main tasks were setting up road blocks to spot enemy agents, and patrolling and protecting airfields and factories. This was not glamorous work, but it had to be done. If there had been no Home Guard, large numbers of regular soldiers would have been tied up in guard duties.

Later on, the Home Guard was given new duties, especially during the Blitz when it was called upon to assist the civil defence services in rescue and clearing up operations. Seven thousand Home Guardsmen were trained in bomb disposal, while 140 000 others served in anti-aircraft units. Many younger members were trained as a mobile defence force, and a special group was organised into a 'secret army' to wage a guerilla war behind enemy lines should the Germans ever occupy Britain.

In all, 1206 Home Guardsmen were killed and another 557 were injured on duty. Most of these casualties were caused by flying bombs and by training accidents. In contrast, the Home Guard inflicted very few casualties on the enemy, although some units did claim to have shot down German aircraft with rifle fire. In fact, the Home Guard proved to be more of a danger to British civilians than to the enemy. Several people were shot by nervous or careless Home Guardsmen manning road blocks:

> *Mrs Margaret Jones was fatally injured early today in a Home Guard shooting tragedy.... [The car] had been passed on and while a sentry was approaching another car going in the opposite direction, his rifle went off and the shot passed through the rear window of the doctor's car.*
>
> *Dr Lewis was struck in the ear by the bullet which afterwards entered Mrs Jones' head.*
>
> *Cambridge Daily News*, 23 August 1940

The Home Guard certainly cannot claim an impressive military record or glorious battle honours. However, it does deserve credit for performing tedious and thankless tasks with little training, few weapons and inadequate resources. To the taxpayer, the cost of each Home Guard soldier was £3 per head per year – just one-fortieth of the cost of a regular soldier before the war. If nothing else, the Home Guard was certainly one of the cheapest armies in history!

8

VICTORY

On 14 August 1945 Clement Attlee, the Prime Minister, broadcast to the nation:

> *Japan has today surrendered. The last of our enemies is laid low.... Here at home you have earned respite from the unceasing exertions which you have all borne without flinching or complaint for so many dark years....Peace has once again come to the world....Long live the King.*

For most people, news of the end of the war in the Far East came as an anti-climax. They had already celebrated the defeat of Germany on 8 May, which had ended the blackout and the threat of further air raids. By August people were worn out and weary. They were preoccupied with the return of loved ones, the repair of their damaged homes, and coping with the continuing shortages. Few people had time to consider whether the war had changed their lives for the better.

In fact, the war produced far-reaching changes in British society. The government was forced to accept new responsibilities for the welfare of its citizens. The British people agreed to make great sacrifices, but only in return for improved social services and a better life at the end of the war. The government started to involve itself in areas such as housing, clothing, diet, health and medical care, which it had largely ignored in the past. In 1942 the Beveridge Report actually accepted that it was the state's responsibility to help its citizens through times of hardship and need. It recommended

Victory celebrations in London, 8 May 1945.

children's allowances and a comprehensive system of insurance which would provide everyone with an old age pension and free medical care. These measures were introduced in the years immediately after the war.

But the war did not produce a revolution in British society. Despite the election of a Labour Government in 1945, power, wealth and privilege remained with the same few people. Although the post-war generation was to enjoy more welfare benefits and a higher standard of living than ever before, the traditional structure of British society remained largely unchanged.

Coursework assignment: the Home Front, 1939–45

The following questions are intended to develop the key skills examined at GCSE.

a) Skill: selection, arrangement and presentation of relevant knowledge

(i) Between 1939 and 1945 the British Government played an increasingly active part in the organisation and direction of the lives of its citizens. Produce a timechart to show some of the important events in this process.

(ii) Having arranged these events in chronological order, now rearrange them in order of importance. Next to each event write a brief note explaining why you consider it to be of more or less importance.

b) Skill: understanding historical terminology and concepts

(i) Pair off each of the following terms with the correct definition.

Terms:
a) Blitz; b) Morale; c) Evacuation; d) Rationing;
e) Mobilisation; f) Propaganda; g) Billeting; h) Conscription.

Definitions:
a) The confidence or optimism that a person or group of people feels in a difficult or dangerous situation.
b) Providing soldiers or evacuees with accommodation.
c) Lightning war, usually including the mass bombing of civilians.
d) Making people join the armed forces.
e) Moving people from a dangerous area to a place of safety.
f) Getting people together to perform a particular activity.
g) Limiting the amount that everyone can have of particular items, to ensure 'fair play' in times of shortages.
h) Information, often false or exaggerated, designed to influence people's opinions and behaviour.

(ii) Write a few sentences on each of these terms explaining their importance to the Home Front in World War II.

c) **Skill: evaluation and interpretation of source material**
Examine the following sources:
a) The poster showing Hitler telling a mother to 'Take them back', on page 17.
b) The ATS recruitment poster on page 50.
c) The Squander Bug poster on page 25.

(i) What do all three sources have in common?
(ii) Briefly explain the original purpose of each of these posters. What can they tell us about life on the Home Front?
(iii) Which poster was likely to be most effective in terms of grabbing people's attention and influencing their behaviour? Explain your choice.
(iv) Do you agree or disagree with the statement that posters are a far more reliable source of evidence than photographs for a historian studying the Home Front in World War II? Use examples of posters and photographs in this book to illustrate your answer.

d) **Skill: empathy**
(i) Assume that you are the artist who drew the two *Punch* cartoons on pages 65 and 66. The editor has just received an angry letter from a reader complaining that the cartoons are unpatriotic and are undermining civilian morale. Write a reply justifying your drawing of the cartoons.
(ii) Explain why most people would have found the cartoons harmless and amusing.
(iii) Who might have found the cartoons offensive?

e) **Skill: analysis of continuity and change**
(i) It has often been claimed that wars accelerate change – that they make things happen more quickly than would have been the case in peacetime. Using examples from this book, explain why you agree or disagree with this claim.
(ii) Compile a list of all the special factors and conditions that produced changes in British government and society in World War II. One obvious example is the bombing of people's homes which forced the government to take a new interest in the shelter and housing of its citizens. Try to think of other examples.
(iii) These factors are called 'change agents'. Which change agent do you think was the most important? Explain your answer.
(iv) In what important ways did British government and society remain unchanged by the war?

Skills grid

Key
U Using the evidence
Q Questions
C Coursework assignment

A Historical skills

1 *Using historical evidence*

	Q	U	U	Q	U	Q	Q	Q	Q	U	Q	Q	Q	Q	U	U	U	Q	Q	Q	U	C
	9	14	18	20	23	25	28	31	33	37	40	41	42	47	49	51	55	59	61	64	66	69
Comprehension of variety of sources	■	■	■	■	■	■	■			■	■						■		■		■	
Distinguishing primary and secondary sources										■												
Extraction of information	■	■	■	■	■		■	■		■	■			■		■	■	■	■	■		■
Evaluation, recognising ★ fact *v* opinion, reliability			■		■		■		■					■	■		■		■		■	■
★ bias											■				■			■			■	
★ importance of origin and context											■						■					■
Recognition of inference and implication in a source	■	■				■		■	■		■		■	■		■	■			■		
Comparison of different sources	■		■		■	■	■			■		■	■			■	■				■	■
Reaching conclusions on basis of this comparison		■			■	■				■		■			■		■				■	
Judgement between opinions										■					■		■				■	
Formation of overview and synthesis of one's own opinion						■		■				■			■			■			■	■

2 *Empathy*

	9	14	18	20	23	25	28	31	33	37	40	41	42	47	49	51	55	59	61	64	66	69
Understanding events and issues from perspective of people in the past	■	■						■	■	■	■		■			■						■

B Historical concepts

	9	14	18	20	23	25	28	31	33	37	40	41	42	47	49	51	55	59	61	64	66	69
Cause and consequence	■			■				■						■	■			■				■
Continuity and change																		■				■
Similarity and difference	■														■	■	■					■
Time, sequence and chronology																				■		■
Conflict and consensus		■																				
Historical vocabulary and terminology																						■

INDEX